D1714821

MS. AFRICA

Books by Louise Crane

MS. AFRICA
Profiles of Modern African Women

THE LAND AND PEOPLE OF THE CONGO

by Louise Crane

MS. AFRICA

Profiles of Modern African Women

J. B. LIPPINCOTT COMPANY   Philadelphia and New York

U.S. Library of Congress Cataloging in Publication Data

Crane, Louise, birth date
  Ms. Africa: profiles of modern African women.

  SUMMARY: Brief biographies of thirteen prominent African women
emphasizing their achievements in their chosen careers. Included are Angie
Brooks, Margaret Kenyatta, and Miriam Makeba.
  Includes bibliographical references.
  1. Women in Africa—Biography—Juvenile literature. [1. Women in
Africa—Biography] I. Title.
CT3750.C73   920.72′096 [920]   72–11767
ISBN–0–397–31446–9

FOR NTUMBA

ACKNOWLEDGMENT

So very many people have contributed to this book that it is impossible to name them individually, as they deserve. However, I cannot fail to mention one without whose help I would certainly have floundered: Brigalia Bam. Though it took considerable effort and persuasion to secure her own story, Brigalia was tireless in her efforts to contact others on my behalf; as one in daily communication with women all over the world, her advice was invaluable and she led me to others who also gave counsel and information unstintingly.

Louise Crane

Contents

Introduction

The women whose stories are told here will probably smile at the title "Ms.," for really it was foreigners, not Africans, who started the custom of addressing women as Mrs., Miss, Madame, or Mademoiselle. Whether or not titles are important, women's liberation has certainly occupied an important place in the lives of all these women, though in general they have been equally involved in battles for freedom in other areas, such as race, religion, culture, self-government. The feminist movement has much to learn from the women of Africa and there may be some surprises. For one thing, many of these outstanding women give credit for their success to the men in their lives —fathers, brothers, husbands—who encouraged them to venture beyond the traditional wife/mother roles.

Of course, it would be very foolish to draw conclusions about African "women's lib" or about African women in general on the basis of these few stories. Because of the limits of time and space, this book can cover only a few of the many remarkable women leaders of Af-

rica; there are many professions and many important countries not
represented here—notably women from French-speaking countries,
business women, some outstanding peasant women. Some stories arrived too late for publication; others may be still on their way. But we
hope to include them in another book soon.

Meanwhile I am deeply aware of my responsibility in introducing
the great women in this volume. Among those solicited personally for
their stories, quite a few were at first reluctant to cooperate, speaking
frankly of their wariness of foreign writers who tend to view Africa
through Western eyes; several remembered unhappy experiences
with "journalistic exploitation." Aside from this, all of them are very
busy women with little time or desire to talk about themselves. So I
am most grateful for their trust and for the time many took to answer
questions and to send pictures of themselves.

Though this is only a sampling and cannot cover even these few
modern heroines as adequately as they deserve, it should leave no
doubt of the fascinating diversity of Africa's women leaders and show
how much we need to learn from them. Each of the women here is
distinguished in at least one field and most are active on many fronts,
often while being wife and mother. They come from a variety of
homes—some deprived, some privileged—but all are commonly dedicated to using their extraordinary gifts in the service of their people as
well as the world community. For some—like the women of South
Africa—such dedication has led to great personal sacrifice, sometimes
prison or exile.

And, of course, African women have not suddenly become outstanding. They have been there all along, for many generations, their
noble deeds sung by African troubadours, but only now getting into
Western history books. They have been a vital part of independence
movements of all the thirty-eight nations that have become free of colonial rule since 1950; progressive male leaders such as President

Nyerere of Tanzania and President Kaunda of Zambia have from the beginning given them important positions in government. Often, however, women have had to fight old-fashioned ideas about their "place," as these stories show.

Those who are so vital to African—and world—life today all pay tribute not only to the women of the past, but to the fathers, mothers, and grandparents who have cleared the path before them.

While African women are moving into new fields, they have not rejected their role as mothers. As these stories show, even the single women, such as Margaret Kenyatta, and those, like Angie Brooks, whose children are grown, feel a deep responsibility for the shaping of young lives. And so the tribute of the Guinean writer, Camara Laye, written while he was a lonely student in Paris, applies to those "career" types as well as to the simpler women who have not roved as far:

> Dark woman, African woman, O mother, I thank you for all you have done for me. . . . Woman of the fields, woman of the streams, woman of the great river, simple woman, patient woman, O mother, I think of you. . . . O Damon, Damon of the great race of blacksmiths, I think of you always. . . . Dark woman, African woman, O mother, I thank you for all you have done for me, your son, so far from you, yet so near! *

---

* Camara Laye, *The Dark Child*, New York, Farrar, Straus and Giroux, 1969.

SIERRA LEONE

LIBERIA

GHANA

NIGERIA

KENYA

ZAMBIA

MADAGASCAR

SOUTH AFRICA

AFRICA

GHANA

Annie Jiagge

and the Women Who Went Before Her:
JULIA BARBARA DE LIMA SEDODE
HENRIETTA LOUISE BAETA

Ghana's court of appeals judge, Mrs. Annie Jiagge, considered one of Africa's great leaders, has a list of accomplishments so long and in so many varied fields that it would take a full-length book to do her justice. But when approached about her story, she responded with two more stories equally interesting: those of her grandmother, Julia Barbara Sedode, and her mother, Henrietta Baeta. Indeed Mrs. Jiagge feels her own life is "not very interesting" compared to theirs. We don't agree, but we do think you will understand Annie Jiagge better after you have heard about the remarkable women who preceded her.

Julia Barbara de Lima Sedode ("Babla")

Julia Barbara de Lima was the daughter of a Portuguese trader named Cezar Cequira de Lima, who came in the middle 1800's to the Gold Coast, the area on the African west coast now known as Ghana. There were few foreigners in this part of Africa at that time other than some traders and a few Christian missionaries. The British had won out over other European countries in establishing commercial claim to the Gold Coast, but until 1901 the fierce fighting Ashanti chiefs kept them from penetrating the interior.

Cezar Cequira de Lima built himself a mansion by the sea at Vodza, near Keta, and settled there. He was married twice to African women and had two daughters, Emilia and Julia Barbara—the latter born in 1858. When he became ill, he went back to Portugal to get cured and left his younger daughter, Julia Barbara, in the care of the Bremen Mission, a German missionary society in Keta. They placed her in the mission boarding school. Cezar Cequira de Lima never recovered but died in Portugal. Before his death he made a will, which was published in the European papers, leaving all his large fortune to his daughters. However, when the inheritance papers came to Keta for the little girls to sign, the German missionaries advised them to reject the fortune, for they said the Portuguese merchant had gained this "blood money" from slave trade. So Barbara and her sister took the advice of the missionaries and returned the papers to Portugal, unsigned.

Left penniless, Barbara continued under the care of the missionaries in Keta. At the school she learned many practical subjects in homemaking which would help her earn her living. At the age of twenty-three she married Christian Sedode, a lecturer at the nearby seminary, and the first African sent to study in Germany. Henrietta,

Mrs. Jiagge's mother, was born the following year, on February 11, 1881.

Although Julia Barbara, or "Mami* Babla" as she was called by the Africans, was only a housewife, she ran a home for training over one hundred women and girls, teaching dressmaking, various kinds of needlework, crochet, knitting, etc. She ran a laundry and was the only one in that area who could launder successfully the stiff clerical collars that the missionaries and African pastors wore. Julia Barbara taught cooking—both African cooking and European cooking. She baked bread and cakes, made sausages, and traded in textiles and beads. Whatever she did was done so well that her name, "Babla," became the household word everywhere for something or someone of highest quality. Through the whole region everyone knew about "Babla." Even today in Ghana, when you hear someone use the word "Babla," you can be sure they are talking about high quality. Women still boast of their mothers' "Babla" breeding—they were in Barbara's home.

Henrietta Louise Baeta

Julia Barbara Sedode had no other children besides Henrietta but, since African children never grow up alone, she adopted a number of children from her extended family to be brothers and sisters to her daughter. All the children were raised in the Sedode household as one family.

While doing research for a book on church history recently, Christian Baeta, Henrietta's son (Mrs. Jiagge's brother), found a great deal of material on the family in the archives of the Bremen Mission in Germany. Henrietta's story, which he extracted and translated from

---

* "Mami"—a title of respect, meaning "Mother."

these papers, follows here in part, with some additional comments by
Mrs. Jiagge:

    Mama Henrietta must have been a very lively and inquisi-
tive child. A letter has been preserved which her father wrote
to one of his friends in Germany asking urgently for some
children's picture books to be bought and sent to him because
Henrietta was doing havoc to his theological books looking for
pictures!

    The family later moved to Keta where Mama started school
as soon as she could go. Her father watched closely over her
studies whilst her mother ensured that she also learnt all the
home duties of a girl. One of the missionary ladies remarked
that she did not know any other African girl on whom so
much loving parental care and attention was lavished as on
Henrietta. Mama often recounted how, after completing the
lower grade school, she went with her father in much fear and
trembling (because no girl had been accepted before) to seek
admission to what was then called the Middle School. The
missionary headmaster, who knew her well, said to her quite
harshly, "What do you want here, Henrietta? All the learning
you will ever need is to be able to do sums about chickens
(*koklo-konta*, i.e., chicken arithmetic) and that you can do already."

    But he did take her on. Her other vivid memory of Middle
School was when one day after school, she encountered one of
the older boys of her class in a lonely lane. He wanted to beat
her up for having got all her sums right at school that morning,
which, he said, a girl should never do. She was greatly terrified
but suddenly some two women turned into the lane and to her

great relief the boy went away shaking his fist and warning that if she ever dared to do that sort of thing again he would show her something!

At 15 she had completed all the schooling available at Keta in those days and was immediately appointed by the Deaconesses as a pupil teacher in the Girls' School, which had only recently opened. . . . There is this description of her teaching by the Chief Deaconess, Sister Hedwig Rohns,

"It was always a special joy for me, during the Religious Instruction period, to go to Henrietta's class and sit on a bench behind her to listen. The eyes of all the children would hang on her lips as if enchanted, and would shine with fullest participation. . . . I often almost wished I could be a little African girl myself, to have the stories narrated to me in such a way."

At the age of 18 years, my mother started the Young Women's Christian Association in Keta in the Gold Coast. . . . It happened this way. My grandfather Christian Sedode was conversing with his wife Barbara one afternoon when she was ironing clothes. He told her about the various activities of the Young Women's Christian Association in Germany and also about the formation of a World Y.W.C.A. My mother, who was helping with the ironing, asked, "Why can't we have a similar organization here?"

Her mother's reply was, "You go and start one."

My mother Henrietta collected her friends together and told them of the YWCA of Germany and the fact that a YWCA started in the Gold Coast could be affiliated to the newly formed world YWCA. Her friends, all of the same age group, were delighted and so it was that nine young African women declared the inauguration of the YWCA in Keta on January

26, 1899. The Constitution adopted by the Association was an interesting one. It laid down strict rules of behavior for members and its purpose was to the full development of young women for service in the Church and to mankind. . . . The new association . . . met in the homes of members in turn until it grew so large that it had to meet in the Mission house. Mercy Baeta (my father's elder sister), a talented musician, taught members songs and how to play the harmonium and the guitar. She taught them songs composed by herself and other Africans but also songs from other nations. The YWCA grew rapidly and its presence was prominent in the whole area. Money was raised from concerts and sale of handwork and the proceeds were used for specific purposes like buying church bells for village churches and so on.

On February 10, 1906, there was a special celebration in the Girls' School to mark both the 10th anniversary of Mama's service as a teacher and her departure to enter married life. The school assembly hall was made festive with palm branches and flowers; the girls recited Biblical and other pieces and sang songs, among them a special one saying "Thank you". . . . The missionary in charge gave an address based on Mama's confirmation text: "For he will give his angels charge of you, to guard you in all your ways. On their hands they will bear you up, lest you dash your foot against a stone." (Psalm 91:11–12). This text in Ewe, which her father had inscribed for her in letters burned into wood, the work of a German art firm, for hanging up in her room, played a very important role in her adult life throughout. In all situations of stress she maintained a simple, child-like trust in the fulfillment of its promise to her. On 19th April, 1906, she was married to the teacher-catechist (and later Pastor) Robert Domingo Baeta in the

church at Keta, and went with him to live in Lomé, Togo,*
where he had been recently transferred.

All my mother's children were born in Lomé in the big
church house with a large garden not far from the Cathedral.
This was my home until my father died in 1943 and we moved
into a new house built by my mother opposite the church
house. My mother had eight children: four boys and four girls;
three of the children died before they were three years of age
and a fourth died when he was twelve.

In Lomé my mother ran a home for girls similar to that of
her mother but on a smaller scale. All her married life she
taught Bible classes and was the leader of various women's
groups. When the wife of one of the early French Governors
of Togoland started a voluntary association of "Togoland
Mothers" ("Mères Togolaises") to help expectant and young
mothers, as well as neglected or deprived children, Mama was
appointed President and very actively led their endeavours
until their service had grown so large that it had to be taken
over by the Government Department of Social Welfare.

In 1930 Mama published in Ewe a brief biography of her
best friend in youth, who had become her sister-in-law, Dada
Mercy Baeta.

Since her husband's death in 1943 her role in the congregation, which had always been considerable, became even more
important. . . . She headed practically all the women's groups.
She was particularly fond of one which she had started for elderly women, who otherwise tended to be left out of things.
They met in her home for Bible study, general fellowship and

* Togo at that time was under German domination. At the beginning of World War I, it was
divided between the English and French; the English section eventually became part of modern Ghana, while the section ruled by the French became the independent republic of Togo
in 1960. Lomé is the capital of Togo today.

singing practice. Whenever they were invited to sing in church their feeble voices would soon be supported by the subdued humming of the rest of the congregation.

Owing to her advanced age her older daughter (Mrs. Jiagge) took Mama to live with herself at Accra, Ho and Tema. At each of these places the church women soon gathered around her for Bible study and fellowship. . . .

Mama lived a full and happy life. . . . She wanted to know and understand everything happening around her and delighted in sharing all the family fun. She took a large part herself in cooking the lunch for her 90th birthday last February (1971) and personally dished it out to all. . . .

She was quite well in health until her son William died. This was the fifth child of eight to die before her. . . . Four days after her son's burial she developed a general weakness which became steadily worse. . . . She died quickly, quietly and peacefully on the eighth day of her illness.

Bless the Lord, O my soul!

Annie Jiagge

With such a background it is hardly surprising that Annie Ruth, sixth-born of the Baeta children, should grow up to become the strong, versatile, and incredibly energetic woman that she is. Wherever she is, be it in her Justice chambers, in a meeting of the United Nations, of the YWCA, or a conference on women's rights, she can be counted on to stir people into practical action. Few women anywhere have managed to be an important part of so many historic events in all parts of the globe. For that matter, few men have achieved so much.

An article in *Time* magazine (August 31, 1970), carrying a picture

Mrs. Annie Jiagge, chairman of the 21st Session of the Commission on the Status of Women, at the UN in January, 1968. Seated at her right are Marc Schreiber and Margaret Bruce of the UN Division on Human Rights.

of Justice Jiagge, dressed in her flowing red judicial robes and curly white British Parliament wig, made this statement:

> Annie Jiagge was Ghana's first woman lawyer, judge and finally Supreme Court justice. She headed an investigation into the corruption of the Nkrumah era that has been hailed as a landmark in African political reform and justice.

Chairman of the United Nations Commission on the Status of Women, president of the Ghana YWCA, vice-president and member of the Executive Committee of the World YWCA, member of the World Council of Churches Division on Inter-Church Aid, member of the Council of the University of Ghana, 1969 winner of the Gimbles' International Award for Humanitarian Work, 1969 winner of the Grand Medal award of the government of Ghana—the list of Judge Jiagge's accomplishments goes on and on.

The early part of her life followed much the same pattern as that of her mother and grandmother. After some early schooling in Lomé, Annie Ruth Baeta returned to her mother's hometown, Keta, so that she could attend the Keta Presbyterian School. Later she went to Accra (capital of Ghana today), where she took teacher training at Achimota Training College. Still later she came back to serve as headmistress of the Keta Presbyterian Senior Girls' School.

But after five years as head of the school, she began to look in new directions.

Things were changing in the Gold Coast and Togo, as they were all over Africa. By the early 1940's Africans had started traveling abroad; many had gone to England, Europe, or America for their education and were disappointed at what they saw when they came home. In their own countries Africans continued to be dominated by foreign white rulers and even the educated had little voice in their own government. By the end of World War II national consciousness had risen so sharply that many young intellectuals were moving toward complete independence from the colonialists. In 1947 Kwame Nkrumah, later to become prime minister of Ghana, had just come back to the Gold Coast with a number of advanced degrees from the U.S.A. and Britain. He became very dissatisfied with the lack of African participation in the government of his country and immediately began agitating for reform. Though it took another ten years to achieve independence from Britain—years during which Nkrumah and other agitators like him were exiled or jailed by British authorities—the winds of change were blowing ever stronger all over Africa.

The African people of the Gold Coast had long been conscious of the value of good education; there were other families like that of Annie Baeta, with an educational tradition of several generations. Now, with the possibility of more African representation in the government it was obvious that the people themselves needed to be ready, with more university education and more specialized training in legal and judicial matters. Local schools tended to emphasize practical subjects for women, such as manual training or homemaking. The University College of the Gold Coast, established in 1948, took some years to develop fully, so most students interested in higher learning went abroad.

In the late 1940's and early 1950's a law career for any African, no matter how well-trained, was most unpromising; but for an African woman such a career was unthinkable. Women in this region were not exactly shrinking violets, as the stories of "Babla" and Henrietta show, but in general their roles were clearly different from those of men. Settling palavers was usually considered a man's job.

But Annie Ruth Baeta came from a line of women pioneers on both sides of her family. Her father's sister, Mercy Baeta—about whom her mother wrote a book—was a famous educator as well as a musician, and was the first African woman missionary in the Gold Coast.

So Annie Ruth, descended from so many breakers of tradition, saw no reason at all why she could not prepare herself to be a lawyer. And naturally, "Babla" woman that she was, she not only became the *first* African woman lawyer of her country, but in an amazingly short time was just about the *best* there was, man or woman!

After receiving an LL.B. degree from the London School of Economics and Political Science, she went on to qualify as a Barrister-at-Law at Lincoln's Inn, also in London. In 1950 she was admitted to the bar in the Gold Coast, practicing law there for the next five years. In 1955 she was appointed district magistrate and in 1957, the year the Gold Coast became the independent nation of Ghana, she became senior magistrate. And so she was thoroughly prepared to join in the exciting job of developing a new nation, one of the first African countries to become independent.

By this time Annie Ruth Baeta had changed her name to Mrs. Annie Ruth Jiagge; her husband, Fred K. A. Jiagge, a university graduate distinguished in his own right, later became managing director of the Tema Development Corporation, responsible for a large share of Ghana's industrial development.

In 1959, only two years after the independence of Ghana, Mrs. Jiagge was appointed a judge of the Circuit Court of Ghana; three years later, in 1961, she was made a judge of the High Court.

Ghana was now setting the pattern for many other African nations just coming into independence; by 1960 it had become a republic and Kwame Nkrumah had moved from prime minister to president of the country. New African leaders, such as Patrice Lumumba of the Congo (now Zaire), journeyed to Accra to consult the man who was fast becoming one of the most powerful figures on the continent. Annie Jiagge and others like her involved in the government of Ghana were proud of their president and supported him in his plans for bringing a better life to all African citizens. However, as Nkrumah grew more powerful and ambitious, he became a dictator, jailing anyone who did not agree with him, spending vast sums of money, without consulting anyone, on projects which were often more for show than for practical use; he called himself "lion," "prophet of Africa," and other such flattering titles. While there were many who praised him for putting Ghana on the map and for making the voice of African people heard in the world, many of his own countrymen were also aware of growing corruption, loss of individual freedom, and waste of government money. In early 1966, while Nkrumah was on a visit to the People's Republic of China and North Vietnam, Ghana was taken over by a military regime; the ousted president had to flee in exile to Guinea. But though he was still in exile when he died in April, 1972, Nkrumah was far from forgotten. Ghana flags flew at half-mast and tributes came in from all over the world. Even those who deplored his mistakes agreed with a statement made by one African leader, "He raised the stature of the black man all over the world."

President Nkrumah left the country in 1966 with serious economic problems, a number of them traceable to corrupt government officials of his regime. The new government appointed a commission headed by Mrs. Justice Annie Ruth Jiagge to investigate the assets of some thirty-three officials who were suspected of having padded their income through influence peddling. The inquiry, known as the Jiagge Commission, involved over three hundred sittings, many conferences, examining hundreds of exhibits, and listening to hours of testimony from the defendants and other witnesses. As one of the reports noted, "Getting a relevant answer from Mr. ——— was a tedious exercise." But everyone had a fair hearing. At the end of the investigation some of the accused were found guilty and were ordered to pay back the government; in other cases the Commission was "satisfied" that assets had been acquired by "lawful income." The five reports, each over two hundred pages long, issued in June, 1969, were hailed as a monument to justice and freedom and Mrs. Jiagge was given major credit.

The same year, 1969, she was made judge of the Court of Appeals of Ghana, the highest honor possible; also that year the government awarded her the Grand Medal.

There was still another significant happening in 1969, for Mrs.

Justice Annie Jiagge.

Jiagge and all the people of Ghana: in August the country had its first free election since the downfall of Nkrumah. There were many who, like Mrs. Jiagge, had been working for this day, believing that no progress could be made against corruption and waste until every citizen, from every hill and village, was consulted and made responsible. On Election Day, August 29, 1969, after many months of listening to candidates from opposing parties, the people of Ghana lined up at voting booths in every corner of the country, some standing many hours to take their turns at deciding who would be the next prime minister. As each voter went through, his palm was marked with deep black lines which could not be washed off for at least a week; thus there was no chance to sneak in and vote twice. Though there were many disappointed candidates the next day, those who had lost sang "funeral" hymns good-naturedly while the victorious supporters of Prime Minister Busia danced in the streets for joy. Unfortunately, less than three years later, in January, 1972, Busia's government, too, was ousted by a military coup, because of its failure to cope with economic problems.

In the years she was gaining recognition at home, Mrs. Annie Jiagge was also becoming a familiar and highly respected figure in such world bodies as the United Nations, the World Council of Churches, and the YWCA. Because of her heritage she had become world-conscious at an early age; by the time of her first appointment as a delegate to the United Nations Commission on the Status of Women, in 1961, she had already traveled to Christian youth and church conferences in England, Norway, the Netherlands, Lebanon, Mexico, the United States, and India.

From the moment Annie Jiagge walked into the UN, things were never quite the same. The UN in New York was already accustomed to distinguished African women—Angie Brooks had been a delegate since 1954—but Mrs. Jiagge attracted special and immediate attention. Physically she was impressive, an attractive, amply built woman, dressed in the colorful robes of her country, dignified, yet very warm and human. Her speeches were direct and to the point; delegates quit wandering around in restless boredom. They settled in their seats, turned on the earphones, and listened attentively to this woman who really had something important to say. In 1966 she made a draft for the UN Declaration on the Elimination of Discrimination Against Women which became a definitive working document; much of Mrs. Jiagge's original wording appeared in the final Declaration adopted by a unanimous vote of the UN General Assembly in 1967.

Nice though it was to have such an important world group agree to eliminate discrimination against women, Judge Jiagge knew that the finely worded Declaration, in English and French, could mean nothing to the wives of Ewe fishermen or Akan cocoa growers. Furthermore, she knew that nothing could really change until the main victims of discrimination—uneducated and voiceless women—could participate, for only they knew what the specific problems were. Bewildering as were the rapid changes brought on by nationalism and industrial development to most ordinary peoples of Africa, it was the women who were most confused and oppressed. Even by their own men they were not valued and respected as they once were, for by the new standards most women were uneducated, misfits in a new society. Opportunities for education, jobs, or anything beyond bearing children or preparing cassava were denied many; nor could they be certain of their homes. A man now could discard his wife as easily as a piece of furniture and no one would care; the old, close-knit community was not there to take her in.

Though, with her unusual endowments and extraordinary family background, Annie Jiagge had herself escaped these problems, she knew they existed for many others. She also believed that African women were capable of bettering their lot if only they could be roused and organized; they must be shaken from their apathy. But until they fully understood what was going on, these women could have no voice in their own destiny.

She soon had a chance to prove her point. In 1968 Judge Jiagge was elected Chairman of the 21st Session of the UN Commission on the Status of Women—the first African to be elected to this office. Soon after, in November of the same year, she organized a seminar in Accra, Ghana, on the Civic and Political Education of Women; this was to serve as a stimulus for all the women in Africa. With what was later quoted as "rare intuitive insight," Mrs. Jiagge brought rural leaders from each of the nine regions of Ghana. Further, in order for them to understand the debates, she arranged for simultaneous interpretation into three Ghana dialects. Now if Mrs. Opoku from Mampong did not understand the loud argument in English between the lady on the platform and the lady in the second row, she could turn on her earphones—a new experience in itself—and hear a version in Twi. If Mrs. Opoku felt like saying something herself, she, too, could speak up in her own language and be sure that everyone would understand her. The women from the villages, the hills, the rivers, all had plenty to say and they demanded action. Things would never be the same again in Mampong, in Keta, or in Sekondi!

This was the first time in the history of the UN that anything like this had been done. Previous regional conferences for women had been held in Ethiopia and Togo, but nothing so well organized, with follow-up plan, at the "grass roots" level. Once encouraged, African women from everywhere spoke up and their united impact on world bodies was staggering! They had always been there, strong female voices in independence movements, energetic crusaders against corruption, capable civil servants, efficient business women, teachers, nurses, doctors; in each country the contributions were impressive, but many people outside had never heard of them. When brought together, through the efforts of Mrs. Jiagge and others like her, their strength was formidable. Indeed at a conference on women's rights in Zambia in 1970 Mrs. Kenneth Kaunda, wife of the president, felt it necessary to soothe the men of Africa at the beginning of her speech (see Gwendoline Konie's story, page 96). At that same conference Mrs. Kaunda quoted as a keynote a "piece of advice given to us by one of the greatest African women leaders . . . Mrs. Annie Jiagge: 'Apathy among women is a sad and unfortunate situation. Every woman can do something—starting from herself. If a woman can whip herself out of apathy, she can help another woman to do the same.' " As she talked to women's groups all over the continent, Mrs. Jiagge urged them not to wait until family commitments were over before they took an active part in public life. Because of the urgency of development on the continent and the low life expectancy in developing countries, she said such delays would mean too great a loss, both economically and culturally.

How does one person find the time to accomplish so much? What keeps Mrs. Justice Jiagge so down-to-earth and human, accessible to anyone who needs her? In spite of all her worldwide honors and recognition, she sees herself only in terms of a job to be done.

Perhaps the key to it all lies in a deep Christian faith inherited from her family but reinterpreted in terms of today's world and with her quite personal. In a day when many people discard religion as an outworn, meaningless thing, Annie Jiagge finds it a live, motivating, and sustaining force, giving her hope when others despair, prodding her to action when others give up without trying. Most of all, it keeps her from taking herself or others too seriously, for, like others who rely on support of Christian faith, she believes, as she said in a recent article,

The future is certainly in God's keeping and under his unique control. Yet God also uses us in fulfilling his purpose. We know that God does not work in all hearts alike but according to the preparation and sensitivity he finds in each of us. The first big issue on each of our agenda for this new decade,

as I see it, is to be prepared for and sensitive to God's work in
our hearts.*

It was this belief that sent the young woman out from her palm-
shaded home on the African west coast some twenty-five years ago,
seeking other sensitive hearts. She found them in all parts of the
world: at the World Conference of Christian Youth in Oslo, Norway, in 1947; and again at Travancore, India, in 1952; at YWCA
meetings in Lebanon, Jordan, England, and Mexico. They gave to
her and she to them and together they are still seeking solutions to the
world's problems within a Christian context. Annie Jiagge's activities
as a churchwoman are far too numerous to mention in detail: a former
vice-president of the World YWCA, she has been a member of its
executive committee for twelve years; an active volunteer in the
World Council of Churches for many years, she attended assemblies
in Amsterdam, Netherlands (1947), Evanston, Illinois (1954), and
Upsala, Sweden (1968); she represented the World Council of
Churches at the Roman Catholic Laity Conference in Rome in 1967
and served from 1968 to 1971 as a member of the Inter-Church Aid
Division of the World Council of Churches.

Justice Annie Jiagge is aware of the fact that she represents in herself a link between several very different worlds: the United Nations
world, which is anything but united on how to solve problems of war,
hunger, and poverty that threaten to engulf us all; the church, which
seems remote and useless to so many people; and the African people,
too little understood and known by the so-called developed nations of
the world. In a recent article entitled, "The Things That Make for
Peace," she simplified it all by referring to the Bible passage where

---

* Justice Annie Jiagge, "What Is Struggling to Be Born?" *Concern*, July–August, 1970, p. 24.

King Solomon asked God for wisdom and understanding rather than for riches and glory:

> The beauty of this passage lies in God's response to the request for a heart to understand how to discern between good and evil. We worry a lot, toil a lot in search for peace, but it looks as if we forget or are ignorant of the first step—the great prerequisite for peace. A heart to understand how to discern between good and evil is the heart capable of removing all areas of conflict and this makes for peace.*

Then, hammering home a point often overlooked by the comfortable and the rich of developed nations, she said,

> International Peace, however, seems to require a cooperative effort—the full collaboration of all nations on earth, the rich as well as the poor. Without effective participation of all nations there can be no lasting peace, and incidentally, very little energy is generated on empty stomachs. This makes some nations too weak to participate effectively.**

Those who have sat with Mrs. Jiagge in world assemblies are awed by her ability to cut through the fat of long, tedious debate. She will listen patiently and quietly for so long, and then, just as the discussion seems hopelessly stalled, she will command the floor and in a few sentences sum up the issue and offer a practical solution.

If you had seen Justice Jiagge in her chambers in Accra, dressed in

* Justice Annie Jiagge, "The Things That Make for Peace," *Christian Teachers' Seminar*, August 7, 1970, p. 22.

** *Ibid.*

Justice Annie Jiagge greets Bishop Martinson, assistant Anglican bishop of Accra.

traditional British judicial style in white wig and flowing red robes, you might be too awestruck to venture near her residence in the same city. However, should you go there, you might be surprised: beyond the surrounding high wall there is an attractive house of modest size, flanked by tropical shrubbery, a garden, and with a backyard full of poultry. No alarm clock can take the place of an African rooster crowing at dawn. A number of loud barking dogs add to the friendly din, and in the midst of it all the world-famous judge bends lovingly over her garden. She is, as she says, "a keen gardener."

In spite of her busy global life, home, family, and friends are very dear to her. Judge Jiagge and her husband are popular guests wherever they are, and like to do their own share of entertaining. African

Mrs. Jiagge's home in Accra.

hospitality, of course, always involves a generous outlay of food. An American woman who was recently visiting Ghana with a group from the YWCA was invited along with the others to a dinner at the Jiagge home. Alarmed at the size of the guest list and feeling she had been invited only because she happened to be with the others—who were old friends—the American declined with a polite excuse. Later she learned from those who did accept the invitation that there were "close to 300" and that it had been a gala affair. The only problem was that the judge insisted on doing the cooking and was so occupied in the kitchen, preparing a specially ordered fish and other African delicacies, that most of the guests never saw her!

Except for her husband, who leads a busy life in Accra and Tema as managing director of the Tema Development Corporation, there is now only one member of her immediate family nearby: her brother Christian, head of the Department of Religion at the University of Ghana, who is due to retire soon. Christian Baeta, too, served many years on the executive committee of the World Council of Churches. A sister, Mrs. Lily Mallet, formerly a schoolteacher, works at the Ghana High Commission in London. William, the brother who died in August, 1971, just preceding the death of Mrs. Baeta, was also involved in international affairs, serving as director of personnel at the International Labor Organization in Geneva, Switzerland. Thus it is easy to see the "Babla" quality has come down to men and women of the third generation and benefited not only Ghana but the world.

Justice Annie Jiagge still insists her own life is "insignificant" and she means it. But all we can say is we feel "Babla" would be most pleased with her granddaughter.

Efua Sutherland

We live close to the spirit of our ancestors in quiet villages they founded on our white shores and in our green forests. A wonderful spirit of community and adjustment to life prevails there which is one of the paths to human progress our fathers found.

. . . But we want to see our land developed and our opportunities increased . . . we want better houses and healthier villages. . . .

All the skill and equipment we need for the material progress can be bought or acquired through hard work. What we cannot buy is the spirit of originality and endeavor which makes a people dynamic and creative.*

These words, from her book, *The Roadmakers*, express the philoso-

* Efua Sutherland, *The Roadmakers*, London, Newman Neame Limited.

phy of Efua Theodora Sutherland, listed inadequately in *Who's Who in Africa* as a "Ghanaian poetess and playwright." Much more than that, she is herself perhaps the best example of what she calls the "spirit of originality and endeavor" that cannot be bought. Lamenting the "least desirable tastes and values of the outside world [which] reach us through the films and junk we import," Mrs. Sutherland has dedicated herself unswervingly for some years to preserving the "spirit of our ancestors," by creating literature and theater that are truly African.

Founder of the Ghana Society of Writers, Ghana Experimental Theater, the Ghana Drama Studio, the Kodzidan (the "Story House," a community project), and Kusum Agoromba (a touring theater company), Efua Sutherland has also written a number of short stories, poems, and plays, for both children and adults, in her mother tongue as well as in English. Though much of her play material has been written for use in the Ghana theater, the works published in English have become well known abroad. Especially popular in America is a delightful children's book, *Playtime in Africa*, which is illustrated with photos by Willis E. Bell, a longtime artistic collaborator and friend of Efua Sutherland.

Though all of her enterprises have been highly praised for artistic significance, their impact on Ghana is much more far-reaching. At a time when traditional values and modern needs have come into conflict, she has helped Africans, literate and illiterate, adapt to change creatively, by giving them outlets for self-expression and also encouraging a deeper sense of community and purpose. While Mrs. Sutherland herself provides the igniting spark and driving force, each of her projects has inspired others: little more than ten years ago, there were no published Ghanaian authors; now, since the formation of the Ghana Society of Writers, there are many. The Kodzidan, Story House Theater, rallied a whole village to self-improvement. Most ex-

citing has been the way in which, through Efua Sutherland's skillful
guidance, many divergent elements have been brought together:
drama students at the University of Ghana, where she is a research
fellow, learn African traditions from the rural community at Atwia,
site of Kodzidan; Greek classics are played in Ghanaian versions; *Everyman*, the ancient morality play, is broadcast on Ghana TV in
Akan, a widely spoken Ghanaian dialect.

The inspirer of all this is a beautiful woman, reserved and somewhat distant with strangers, but warm to those she accepts as friends.
Though Mrs. Sutherland shuns publicity for herself, everyone who
comes to Ghana naturally hears about her. In 1966 the American
Broadcasting Company television crew doing a documentary on Africa went to Atwia because of the Story House project and did a film
on the dramatic life of the community. *Time* magazine, in an article
on African women (August 31, 1970), featured several distinguished
Ghanaians, among them Annie Jiagge and Efua Sutherland.

People who have met Mrs. Sutherland almost always speak of her
in theatrical terms, each one remembering a particularly vivid scene.
One American recalls waiting for a long time in the open courtyard
of the playwright's home; when Efua Sutherland finally appeared, she
was so compellingly regal in her bearing that the visitor was confused
as to whether to bow or to applaud. Another visitor remembers Mrs.
Sutherland sitting pensively by a tree outside the newly completed
theater in Accra, considering where to place some symbolic works of
art.

Mrs. Ruth Sloan, an American long associated with African affairs,
speaks of her thus: "I consider Efua Sutherland one of the three greatest women I have been privileged to know. The others are Eleanor
Roosevelt and Helen Suzman." (Helen Suzman is the lone member
of an opposition party in the South African Parliament, celebrated for
her open criticism of "apartheid.")

Efua Sutherland at home.

Since it is impossible within these few pages to give a complete picture of this remarkable woman, we will skip only briefly over her earlier life and concentrate, as she would prefer, on her work of the past fifteen years as a leader in Ghana's literary and theatrical development.

She was born at Cape Coast, Ghana, on the palm-lined west coast of Africa, on June 27, 1924. Although Cape Coast has recently become known as the site of the fast-growing University of Cape Coast, tourists have been going there for some years to see the old slave-trading castles, Elmina and Cape Coast, built before Columbus discovered America. It is also one of the historically important homes of the Fante people, long considered one of Ghana's most colorful groups.

Her name Efua is a traditional Fante name for a girl born on Friday. It is the custom of her people to perform a naming ceremony— "outdooring"—on the eighth day after a baby's birth. At the ceremony a father formally names his child after a respected ancestor. The ancestral name Efua inherited at her naming ceremony is Nyankoma (Gift of God). Theodora, which means the same, is her baptismal name, and it is interestingly explained by the fact that the Christian church used to regard African names as non-Christian, and therefore not acceptable for baptism.

After training in St. Monica's School and Training College in Ghana, Efua Theodora completed further studies in England: at Homerton College, Cambridge, and the School of Oriental and African Studies, University of London.

Returning to Ghana, she taught, from 1951 to 1954, at her alma mater, St. Monica's Training College, Mampong-Ashanti, and at Fijai Secondary School, Sekondi. In 1954 she married an Afro-American, William Sutherland, by whom she had three children: Esi Reiter, Muriel Amowi, and Ralph Gyan.

Though literature and writing had always interested her, it was mostly her teaching experience and concern for the development of her own children that impressed Efua Sutherland with the need for written literature that was truly African. Accustomed to transmitting their own ideas through the oral tradition, Africans generally tended to associate Western ideas with written literature. Even though Ghanaians were generally more advanced in education than Africans of some other countries—some families in Ghana had three generations of education—their schooling was almost a direct, little modified, import from Britain. A sprinkling of conscious individuals apart, most people didn't seem to think it particularly strange that African children learning to read could find only stories about fair-haired white children quite different from themselves. Besides pointing out that there was an appalling scarcity of books in English and the Ghanaian languages either written by Ghanaians or having African inspiration, Mrs. Sutherland noted that most of the people did little reading outside of required textbooks, simply because there was little in the books available to interest them.

Obviously something had to be done and she did it. In 1957, the year Ghana gained its independence from Britain, Efua Sutherland organized the Ghana Society of Writers. By 1958 the society had increased its membership from fourteen to fifty-four writers and had drawn up a program of action. First on the list was a "books on Africa exhibit," which, while inadequate and containing not a single children's book in English written by a Ghanaian, served to point up the need.

"When the first children's book by a Ghanaian is published I shall die happy," declared Mrs. Sutherland to a friend visiting Ghana in 1958. A very short time later her own *Playtime in Africa*, as well as works by other Ghanaian writers, had been published. And today

Efua Sutherland and her daughter Amowi.

publishers' lists everywhere advertise books and plays in various African languages as well as in English, and Ghanaian authors are frequently reviewed by the international press.

It was natural that Mrs. Sutherland and other writers should turn to the traditional storytellers for inspiration. Though theater as conceived by Europeans has not been in the African tradition, storytelling and festival performances have always involved fascinating dramatization. Here is how Efua Sutherland describes an organized group telling an Ananse story (in Ghana a large number of folk stories are associated with the name of Ananse, a fictitious character commonly symbolized as a spider):

> An Anansesem performance by such a group begins with an opening lyric and signs off with another. A story-teller steps into the ring and eloquently delivers his story. He may himself sing the poetic sequences in his story with choral support from the group; or a poet-songster from the group may interrupt the narration . . . with a song contribution which aptly comments on some event in the story, or stresses an effect. Sometimes, the interruption comes from an actor who plays some of the scenes painted verbally by the narrator. Dancing may also be contributed by special dancers from the performing group, or by members of the audience.

In order to study the folklore art, Mrs. Sutherland began attending local funerals—where entertainment for the vigil was customary—as well as other traditional ceremonies. From a group of professional women storytellers, who were engaged for these events, she learned the spoken and musical material and the acting techniques of story-telling. Later she cast some of the women, along with other people recruited from the shops and streets, literate and nonliterate, in some theatrical productions. She also started a children's theater program.

Though the traditional folktales were a natural source for plays, Mrs. Sutherland also found the ancient Greek theater very compatible to Africans, with its similarities in form and theme. Her adaptation of a Greek play, using a Ghanaian chorus, was an instant success.

Mrs. Sutherland had been encouraged in the early stages of her efforts by modest contributions from her personal friends. In 1959 a small grant from Ghana's Ministry of Information enabled her and her companions in the Ghana Society of Writers to launch a literary

magazine called *Okyeame (Spokesman)* for new creative writing. By
late 1959 her experimental theater and writers' workshop programs
had caught the attention of the Fund for Tomorrow Incorporated and
the Rockefeller Foundation, and both organizations contributed funds
to help her develop her work. She decided that the best way to use
this money was to build a center for training Ghanaians in the various
fields of theater as well as for continuing the experiments she had
started for developing indigenous drama. That project required more
money than she had, but the government of Ghana came readily to
her aid, providing the supplementary funds through the Arts Council,
the official organization for the promotion of artistic development.
Thus began the building of the Ghana Drama Studio in Accra, capital
of Ghana.

The first phase of the project, an open-air studio with covered stage
and changing rooms, was completed and formally opened in October,
1961. The design of the building is modern yet has strong traditional
touches. At either side of the entrance to the studio are two Akuaba
dolls, one male and one female, traditional symbols of creativity,
which were carved by Dr. Oku Ampofo, one of Ghana's leading
sculptors. (These dolls are also the symbols for Kusum Agoromba,
the traveling theater group organized in 1968.) The Drama Studio's
symbol is one of the Adinkera designs so well known in Ghana. This
one, called *Mate Masie*, consists of four circles in a cloverleaf arrange-
ment, and has the meaning: "What I hear I contain."

From a distance the Drama Studio appears as a low, white building,
simple and elegant, with a few trimmings in black. Visitors are struck
by the size of the open-air auditorium which can seat as many as 350
people, and by the adaptability of the building for all kinds of staging.
The entrance to the studio is shaped like a traditional Ghanaian stool.
Mrs. Sutherland felt that since most of Ghana's social activities, such
as the naming of a new baby ("outdooring") and storytelling, take

place in a courtyard, it was logical that the Ghana Drama Studio should take the form of a courtyard.

The Studio was officially opened in October, 1961, by the first president of the Republic of Ghana, Dr. Kwame Nkrumah. That year a staff, headed by a director, another Ghanaian playwright, Joe de Graft, was appointed to take charge of the Studio's activities. Many new things began to develop, including the formation of a Studio Players Company which began giving regular performances. In 1963, after the studio program was well launched, Mrs. Sutherland, who had up to now remained independent, accepted an appointment as Research Fellow in Literature and Drama in the Institute of African Studies of the University of Ghana. At this time she transferred ownership of the Ghana Drama Studio to the university so that it could be used as an extension division of the School of Music and

Entrance to the Ghana Drama Studio.

WILLIS E. BELL

Kusum Players leaving the Ghana Drama Studio.

Drama which had just been set up. For a while all the university classes in drama and theater studies were connected at the Studio, but later this proved to be impractical because of its distance from the university campus. (The university is located at Legon, some miles outside Accra.)

From the moment of its opening the Ghana Drama Studio extended its facilities to the general public, to schools and various dramatic groups which sprang up in suddenly theater-conscious Ghana. In a publication by the Ministry of Information (*The New Ghana*, Vol. I, No. II) plans for further development of the Studio and its program were announced:

> The plan includes a modest covered theatre which can be used throughout the year for certain kinds of experimental production, hostel facilities for visiting artists or those attending drama workshops and a park for the production of pageants.

. . . The Studio is intended to stimulate experiments in new forms of Ghanaian theatre, to provide a centre for the training of actors and an outlet for Ghanaian playwrights.

Having started all this, Efua Sutherland was naturally a leading spokesman for the National Theater Movement in Ghana. In 1965 she issued a twenty-five-page review of this movement, entitled "The Second Phase." In the report she analyzed and summarized the accomplishments of the first "nearly ten years" of the theater movement and projected plans for the future, emphasizing particularly the need for more creative material, for professional training, for regional and national companies, and for cultural exchange within Ghana.

Among the many creative enterprises Efua Sutherland has so successfully undertaken, none has been more exciting than the building of Kodzidan (the Story House) in the village of Atwia.

Atwia is a small Fante village in the Ekumfi District of the Central Region of Ghana, seventy-two miles away from Accra, with a population today of close to seven hundred. By self-taxation and communal labor the village of Atwia built a simple school for its children on the best site available. But with limited prospects of higher education and employment, many of the older children tended to leave school and drift to the city.

Mrs. Sutherland's first encounter with Atwia is best told in her own words:

As a Research Fellow of the Institute of African Studies, I arrived at Atwia in January 1964 on the trail of oral literature. The village's reputation for story-telling drew me there, and I went with the single aim of collecting folk-tales. I found a more exciting story-telling tradition than I expected. Over and above that, I found a whole cluster of the oral literature of the Fante in vital circulation there. But the most important discov-

ery was the vitality of the spirit of the community in a depress-
ing environment of poverty and deprivation.

I decided to associate with the village on a long term basis
and my decision was strengthened by the discovery during the
first four months of an extraordinary spirit of enterprise in the
community and its leadership, the Chief, Nana Okosampa VI
(a lady) and the Elders of her court who constitute the Village
Council and Development Committee.

As she settled into the village, she began to see ways of helping the
community solve its problems, the first project being the building of a
place for the village's performances. Using her research funds to establish a community fund, it was possible to buy the materials needed
—such as cement, wood, roofing materials, and to pay for the services
of one mason and one carpenter. These were the only paid workers.

The community organizing itself in an impressive way, supplied all the labour. Children collected pebbles for mixing concrete; the men headloaded bags of cement over a distance of
$1\frac{1}{4}$ miles to the lagoon below the village where water and sand
were available, and headloaded the cement blocks they made
there back to the village; the women headloaded water and
sand from the distance to the building site and helped their
men with the labour chores there. On week-ends the sons of
the village who were carpenters and masons working in Accra
went in relays to Atwia to lend a helping hand to the project.

For eighteen months the construction work proceeded. It
taught the community about building to a plan on proper foun-
dations. But even more important, the project brought to the
surface several issues on attitudes which taught lessons . . . invaluable for subsequent undertakings.

The people chose to call the building Kodzidan (The Story House), thus connecting it with their story-telling art. It was completed in June, 1966. Steadily, since then, this place has become much more than the performance centre it was meant to be.

The Kodzidan, like most houses in Atwia, was built with an inner courtyard partially open to the sky; it was modeled partly after the Kona Clan House, but its design was also influenced by local methods of staging performances both indoors and outdoors. Willis Bell, Mrs. Sutherland's collaborator, drew up the final plans and supervised technical details of construction.

Several times during the construction period groups of drama and literature students from the University of Ghana were brought to Atwia for live seminars. Thus the people of the village got a foretaste of what their center could be.

In July, 1966, one month after Kozidan was completed, the International Folk Music Conference, meeting at the University of Ghana, came out in a body to Atwia to see performances at the new building. Nana Okoampa, Lady Chief of Atwia, welcomed the 150 delegates from all over the world. Detailed program notes in a brochure decorated with a spider web, Ananse's symbol, enabled the audience to follow the fascinating variety of music, dance, and storytelling from a number of neighboring areas. Performers included matrons, elders, and children of Atwia, as well as special ensembles. Last on the program was a "Bodey" group, playing a type of music blending Western and traditional African music, which had become particularly popular with the Ghana youth in the early 1930's; this was a forerunner of the modern "highlife" music. Describing this Bodey music as "rich and capable of infecting the stablest temperament with intemperate buoyancy," the program notes invited the delegates to join in the performance at this point. Dance they did, with joyous abandon!

The villagers were heartened by the enthusiastic response of the foreigners and set to work making other improvements at Atwia. Some of the sons of Atwia who were workers in Accra got together to raise contributions to improve toilets. A woman of one of the major clan houses decided to rebuild her family's clan house. Between September and October, 1966, the entire village participated as the cast for a television film for the American Broadcasting Company and were given a modest fee for their performance. With this money the Kodzidan Fund was established, added to from time to time by earnings from other performances and from donations.

With the establishment of the fund, it was possible to meet some other community needs: e.g., some new classrooms were added to the school; a small community shop was set up to make it easier for people to get basic commodities like kerosene, sardines, sugar, milk, malaria pills, aspirin, and washing soap.

The problem of school leavers—those who complete elementary level education but cannot go any further for various reasons—and drift of youth from the country to the city, plaguing Ghana as much as other countries of the world, was acute in Atwia. But with the new vitality and increasing hope inspired by the Kodzidan, the youth of the village started having second thoughts about leaving. A group of teen-age school leavers organized a theater ensemble of their own, called the Kodzidan Concert Party, creating their own plays in a musical style popular in Ghana. Taking performances to nearby villages, within walking distance or accessible by boat from the nearby lagoon, they began to earn a little money of their own. This inspired them to look for other moneymaking projects. One boy found a way of making hats from the fiber of a dwarf date palm growing in abundance in the region. Within a short time a group had formed around him, making and selling handcrafted hats, bags, and other items; a few took up blacksmith crafts, another, masonry. A community farm project also developed, specializing in growing corn and coconuts. In 1968 a young man who had left the village to work in another area returned to Atwia and used his savings to set up a corn-mill plant for processing corn for Atwia and three other villages in the neighborhood.

New performing groups appeared at the Story House. In 1969 a group of four-to-eight-year-old children sprang up with a musical performance entirely directed by a twelve-year-old leader. There is now a junior storytelling group.

At the first annual village festival following the completion of the Story House, in September, 1966, the people of Atwia demonstrated their acceptance of Kodzidan by officially inaugurating it as a Festival Rite. It has been celebrated this way every year since.

Summarizing her thoughts about the Atwia project today, Mrs. Sutherland says:

> Besides finding a tremendous sense of the performing arts in this village, I also found impressive qualities of leadership. "Soul" is no mystery to the people of Atwia; they breathe it, and live by it in a relaxed unself-conscious way on a daily basis. . . .
>
> I have had a long-standing hunch that the educated African had better *get with* the uneducated communities which form the bulk of his society in every African country at present. Atwia is a place which has inspired me and permitted me the privilege of finding out what this *getting with* MEANS. For a start we have built what the people have named a Story House. It is a place which stands at the heart of the village, and which has become a centre for soul sessions of the people's own performing arts.
>
> Out of the Story House is developing a real community development program which is setting its own natural pace of ev-

olution. Atwia's next objective is to get pure drinking water from the possible sources which are $1\frac{1}{2}$ miles away from an underground spring and $\frac{3}{4}$ of a mile away from a salt water lagoon into which a fresh water river flows.

In January, 1968, Efua Sutherland founded Kusum Agoromba (Kusum Players), a full-time professional drama company based at the Ghana Drama Studio, touring performances in towns and villages throughout the country. In its brochure, decorated with photos of the company's Akuaba symbols and Ananse's spider web, Kusum Agoromba lists as its objective the presentation of "quality plays" to schools at all grade levels, to teachers, the general public, and to such specialized audiences as "church congregations, clubs and associations, the work-force of a business company." It also offers teaching demonstrations for Training College students and teachers with special interest in drama. The company's repertoire of some ten plays (seven of them by Mrs. Sutherland) has an interesting variety: plays on folk or traditional themes; *Odasani*, a Ghanaian version of *Everyman*; *Yaa Konadu*, an African adaptation of Anton Chekhov's *Proposal*; and several musicals, including one based on a Ghanaian novel.

Kusum Agoromba made its performing debut on Palm Sunday, April 7, 1968, with a presentation of *Odasani* in the Roman Catholic Holy Spirit Cathedral in Accra. According to one observer, the play, which was given in the Akan language, "was a magnificent production which came across triumphantly to the English speaking audience." It was presented several months later on Ghana Television. In the playbill for the church presentation, *Odasani (Everyman)* was introduced as "part of a service for your Church," with suggestions for following it with a short sermon on the theme of the play and hymns. Whether given for church audiences or for the general public, this African version of *Everyman* reached everyone with its universal theme.

A scene from Odasani (Everyman).

Describing the debut performance in the cathedral, an American observer noted Mrs. Sutherland's use of a semicircular set, "tightly constructed so that one scene could move to another scene in different settings without interruption in its hour and ten minute production." This observer went on further to comment:

Mrs. Sutherland has chosen actors with dramatic talents, apparent discipline and, in Twi (a version of Akan), power to enunciate their parts. In any language their acting is powerful and has meaning. Mrs. Sutherland knows the Ghanaian so well that she knows which of them to choose and uses existing institutions such as the church for a setting or additional settings as the group moved around Accra and across the country. . . . The members of the company have been drawn from many walks of life. . . . They cannot be this good without devoting their entire time to it. Also to be of importance to Ghana and the people of Ghana they must travel outside of Accra.

Money is an ever-present problem. Although the company has continued to work toward self-support through gate receipts, this goal has not yet been reached so funds must come from other sources to keep it alive. Just as in the past, Mrs. Efua Sutherland, with her resourcefulness, can be counted on to come up with still new ideas and solutions.

Efua Sutherland has never lost sight of her original goal to build up the African literature of Ghana, and for her own contributions to this she still relies heavily on traditional sources:

> I am collecting and studying oral literature because of the very important part such material plays in the lives of the vast majority of people in present day Ghana. From observing the use of this material in performance and its effectiveness in human communication, I am also getting inspiration for approaches to theatre, and for the play I write.

A listing of Mrs. Sutherland's works will be out of date by the time this book is printed, but here are some of those that are currently available in English:

Produced and Published Plays

You Swore an Oath (A storytelling drama, English version published by *Presence Africaine*)

Foriwa (A three-act community play), Ghana Publishing Corporation, Accra

Edufa (A three-act tragedy), Longmans, Green and Co., London; Hill and Wang, New York

Two Rhythm Plays—*Vulture Vulture* and *Tahinta* (children's drama), Ghana Publishing Corporation, Accra

Ananse and the Dwarf Brigade (Ananse play for children), going into publication in Fante and English

Other Published Works

Poems and short stories in several anthologies (*Modern African Prose, Black Orpheus, Voices of Ghana, African/English Literature, Messages*, and others)

The Roadmakers (A study of Ghanaian essences, with photographs by Willis E. Bell), Newman Neame Ltd., London

Playtime in Africa (A book on play life of Ghanaian children, with photos by Willis E. Bell), Atheneum Publishers, New York

Other plays which have been produced include *Odasani, The Marriage of Anansewa*, and several storytelling dramas; *Tweedledum and Tweedledee*, a children's play; *Children of the Man-Made Lake*, a drama for children produced on tape. Other works going into publication or in preparation at the time of this writing are: a big collection of Ghanaian folktales; *The Female Impersonator* (a study of the Ghana Concert Party Theater, fully illustrated); *Makers of the Ghanaian Theater* (a series on notable Concert Party Theater artists); *Studies in African Drama* (a series of papers on the content of African drama); and a play dealing with slavery.

People unfamiliar with African languages often miss the real poetry
of the original literature, whose special sound effects and rhythms are
generally lost in translation; also so much that is intuitive to those who
have lived with African thought media is impossible to "explain" to
outsiders. But Efua Sutherland comes near bridging that gap for foreigners; she has a rare gift of somehow preserving African style and
feeling in English. In this poem she lifts the curtain on a scene familiar
to all who have visited the palm-lined coast of Ghana, which is her
home:

As Fishermen Go to Sea

They grip, they lift their paddles,
They rise a little, they raise a song,
They settle to dip their paddles
Deep in the heaving sea.

They heave off shore, away and away
From the strand of sand,

   Away and away

From the tiptoe standing town
From mothers, children, friends.

   May they return
   May they return
   May they return
To mothers, children, friends.

Gripping and lifting their paddles,
Rising a little, raising a song,
Settling to dip their paddles
Light in the white-foam sea.

LIBERIA

Angie Brooks

"Dimples and dynamism" read the captions of *Newsweek*'s article of September 29, 1969, pairing photos of two prominent ladies attending the General Assembly of the United Nations. "Dimples" referred to Shirley Temple Black, the onetime Hollywood child star, "still dimpled and doll-faced at 41," now making her debut as a diplomat. "Dynamism" referred to the lady who upstaged her, Angie Brooks (also forty-one), "an amply upholstered, motherly-looking lawyer from Liberia . . . the woman who was chosen as president of the 24th session of the UN General Assembly."

"After the overwhelming vote (113 of 118 ballots) in her favor," continued *Newsweek*, "Miss Brooks sailed unhurriedly up the aisle of the Assembly, resplendent in blue and white robes and a silken turban. Swinging an enormous red and black handbag, she climbed the stairs to the podium, heartily embraced a UN official who guided her to her chair, and took her place next to Secretary-General U Thant. Then, after acknowledging the ovation of the delegates, Angie

Brooks—the first African woman to serve as Assembly president—let them have it.

" 'The UN,' said the new Madame President, 'has suffered a decline in prestige in recent years because of its lack of dynamism. Our weakness,' she told the delegates, 'seems to lie in the fact that we all too often view world affairs somewhat parochially, as if they were being played out at the headquarters on the East River of New York. We have sometimes failed to realize that neither oratory nor agreements between delegates nor even resolutions or recommendations have had much impact on the course of affairs in the world at large.' "

Then she bluntly told the delegates they should spend less time congratulating each other on so-called diplomatic "victories" and try more to get their home governments to behave responsibly in the world community.

To some of the newer delegates Miss Brooks's deflating plain talk must have been a bit shocking, but UN veterans were not at all surprised. They knew her as a woman who always goes after what she wants with little or no regard for diplomatic convention. They also knew Angie Brooks as a woman of deep concern and belief in the organization she had helped to nurture for some fifteen years.

Since the age of eleven, when as a self-taught typist she was earning money copying legal documents, Angie Brooks had been a trailblazer: first practicing woman lawyer in Liberia, first woman and first African to serve as president of the UN Trusteeship Council, and now in 1969 the first African woman and second woman (Mme. Pandit of India had been the first) to serve as UN president. Asked how she felt about taking on the demanding job of presiding over the world assembly, "I am proud for my continent, my country and my sex," she said, and then, with a wink, "Not bad for a woman, eh?"

But an *Ebony* account of the event (January, 1970) quoted an experienced African diplomat as saying that though this was "a matter

Miss Angie Brooks, president of the General Assembly, received Brazil's highest award, the Order Nacional do Cruzeiro do Sue, *in her office at the UN.*

that was decided at the level of presidents and kings, Angie Brooks was selected not because she is a woman or a Liberian, but because she is Angie Brooks."

"Being Angie Brooks," said *Ebony*, "is no simple matter."

In addition to many other UN assignments, Miss Brooks has served her own country, Africa's oldest republic, in a number of top posts: counsellor-at-law to the supreme court, assistant attorney general and assistant secretary of state, a post she still holds today; she ran the country once for nearly two weeks when former President Tubman was away from Liberia. Also she has served as professor of law at Liberia, held various posts with the International Federation of Women Lawyers, and with the National Liberian Political and Social Movement. A Baptist, she has since 1966 done special supervisory work for the Lott Carey Baptist Mission, supported by a group of American black churchmen. Miss Brooks has been decorated by at least a dozen governments, including Liberia, China, Cameroon, Yugoslavia, and West Germany, and has received honorary degrees and citations from universities and organizations all over the world. She holds no less than six degrees, including several doctorates of law.

"She started with nothing," says a close friend, "but look at her now."

It is true that Angie Brooks had little going for her in the beginning and she is not ashamed to admit that she earned some of the degrees that advanced her while scrubbing floors and washing dishes. But even as a small girl, living in meager circumstances and with the most limited opportunities, she set her sights high.

"I always wanted to achieve the highest there was," she told an *Ebony* reporter during an interview in 1970.

Angie Elizabeth Brooks was born on August 24, 1928, in Virginia, Montserrado County, Liberia. She was one of nine children of a back-country minister of the African Methodist Episcopal Zion Church. Neither of her parents belonged to the elite "honorables," the descendants of freed slaves who returned to Africa from America and founded the republic of Liberia in 1847, who still dominate the country's social and political life. "Brooks" is an anglicized version of her father's tribal (Grebo) name; her mother came from two other African tribes, the Mandingo and the Vai. Since her parents were too poor to care for all their children, Angie Elizabeth was raised in a foster home in Monrovia, capital of Liberia. Her foster mother was a widowed seamstress, active in the Methodist Church.

Educational opportunities for any girls in Liberia at that time were very limited, but Angie opened some doors of her own. By the time she was eleven years old she had taught herself to type and was earning money copying legal documents. This started her lifelong interest in law. To pay her way through high school she did typing in the afternoons for the Treasury Department and later became a stenotypist for the Justice Department. As she recalled in an interview:

> I always thought, while I was taking records in the court, that the laws could be improved and that, if I could become a lawyer, I might go into the legislature where I would be in a position to help make those laws.*

Since there were no law schools in Liberia, the only way for anyone to study law was to tutor under a practicing lawyer and then qualify by taking a bar examination. Angie Brooks found a lawyer who was willing to teach her, Clarence Simpson, later to become foreign minister for Liberia. The text he recommended for her studies was Blackstone's *Commentaries*, a volume so huge that as she lugged it to her lessons people in the street laughed at her. Another woman who had qualified to practice law was given such a hard time by the men during her first day in court that she walked out of the court-

---

* *Ebony*, January, 1970, p. 30.

room, never to return. But Angie Brooks was not one to let such prejudice stop her.

She had married when she was only fourteen and had two sons; soon divorced, she was left with the additional burden of supporting her children. Although she worked hard at several jobs she could not save enough money to pay for the legal education she wanted. The pastor of the Baptist church, which she attended regularly, recommended that she write to an old classmate of his who was now head of Shaw University, a school for blacks in Raleigh, North Carolina. In her letter to the president of Shaw, Miss Brooks—she had resumed her maiden name after the divorce—said she would be willing to do anything to pay for her education, from scrubbing floors to typing. He accepted her application, but she still had to figure out a way to pay for the long expensive trip to America. With her never-ending resourcefulness, she appealed to no less a person than the president of her country, President William V. S. Tubman.

"In Liberia, the President's office is open to all," she told a reporter of the *New York Post* (September 20, 1969). "I kept plaguing him. I heard he likes to walk at 6, so early one morning I went to see him again." Her persistence so impressed Tubman that he arranged to finance her journey to the United States.

With $25 in her pocket she arrived in Raleigh, North Carolina, and enrolled at Shaw University. While earning her way through by cleaning, cooking, and washing dishes, she excelled at her studies and impressed her fellow students so much that they invited her to join Alpha Kappa Alpha, a black sorority; several years before this sorority had given an honorary membership to Mme. Pandit of India, Miss Brooks's predecessor as woman president of the UN. But outside the school Angie Brooks had a quite different experience. One day when she boarded a public bus in Raleigh she was ordered to take a seat at the back. Bewildered by the order, when she saw many empty seats at the front, she explained to the driver that she would get sick sitting at the rear. But to him she was just another black woman and there was no place for her but the back. She did become ill.

"I didn't think human beings would act like that to other human beings," she said afterward. From that time on—even after Martin Luther King's boycott movement forced the end of such segregation —Miss Brooks traveled only by car when in the South. Some years later the city of Raleigh honored her by giving her keys to the city.

In 1949 Angie Brooks left Shaw with a B.A. degree in social science and went on to study law at the University of Wisconsin. Three years later she had two more degrees, an LL.B. and an M.Sc. in political science and international relations. She had done this by sometimes going without food, working as an assistant in the law library during the day and as a nurse's aide at night. Then she spent two more years doing graduate work in international law at the University College law school of London University.

When she returned to Liberia in 1953, eminently qualified, she was admitted as a counsellor-at-law to the supreme court. When she was asked whether she wanted to work in the State Department or the Justice Department, she chose the latter.

"I selected the Justice Department," she said, "because I wanted to inspire women to enter the field of law. Of course, as assistant attorney general I did do some practicing—prosecuting criminal cases in the courts. This was fine, for young women then did go to school, graduate and study law."

She helped to found a department of law at Liberia University and served as a professor there from 1954 to 1958.

In 1958 President Tubman, to whom she remained staunchly loyal up to the time of his death in 1971, appointed her assistant secretary of state. Later that year, while the president and the secretary of state were both out of the country, she ran the government for ten days.

It was while she was on a visit to the States in 1954 that her long and distinguished career with the United Nations began. A vacancy

Miss Angie Brooks and Secretary-General U Thant at the presentation of a ma-hogany table to the United Nations from Miss Brooks's countrymen.

in the Liberian UN delegation had just occurred and she was asked to fill in at the last minute. She has been a delegate every year since, filling any number of important posts before the crowning achievement of UN president in 1969: in 1956 she was vice-chairman of the General Assembly's Fourth Committee (involved with trust and non-self-governing territories); in 1961, vice-president of the committee on information from nonself-governing territories, as well as chairman of the Fourth Committee; in 1962, chairman of the United Nations Commission for Ruanda-Burundi; in 1964, chairman of the UN visiting mission to the trust territory of the Pacific Islands. In 1965 she became vice-president of the Trusteeship Council, the UN's watchdog over its trust territories, and the following year she was its president. She was the first woman and the first African to serve in this capacity.

During these years Miss Brooks had acquired several more degrees: a doctor of laws from Shaw University and Howard University, in 1962 and 1967 respectively, as well as a doctor of civil law degree from Liberia University in 1964.

Since it is customary for the UN presidency to be shifted each year to a representative of a different geographic area, 1969 was Africa's turn. Only two other Africans had held the post previously, and there had been only one woman president in the history of the UN (Mme. Pandit in 1953).

Angie Brooks was not the slightest bit coy about her desire to have the job. She announced that she believed she would be an excellent candidate and set out to campaign vigorously, visiting some twenty-three countries in Africa because in order to win, she had to have the backing of all forty member states from her continent. Nevertheless her campaign proved successful, for when the votes were counted she had won 113 out of the total 118 cast.

"Our Miss Brooks," as many of the delegates called her fondly, after a popular television heroine, presided over the General Assembly sessions with the efficiency for which she had become known, her style an odd mixture of feminine charm and shrewd diplomacy. Having given the delegates a straightforward but motherly scolding for their failures in past sessions, she tried to eliminate as much idle speechifying as possible from the long, knotty debates. In the middle of one committee meeting she politely cut off Soviet Ambassador Malik in a routine debate, ordered a vote, and went on to new business.

Secretary of state and chairman of the Liberian delegation to the twenty-fourth session of the General Assembly congratulates Miss Angie Brooks on her election as president of the General Assembly.

"Angie Brooks is tough, resilient, patient and unfailingly good-humored," remarked a friend, and it was obvious that she needed to be all of these for her demanding job. She could also be surprisingly gentle. Replying to an interviewer's comment on this aspect of her diplomacy, "That is the way one must be," she answered in pleasantly accented Liberian English, adding a warm and utterly feminine smile. "First you must be soft and let it seem they are having their own way. Then you come down hard on them." *

But Miss Brooks is not simply the wheeler-dealer egotist she might appear to be from these remarks. She is extremely generous, likely to

* *Ebony*, January, 1970, p. 29.

bestow gifts unexpectedly and spontaneously on both friends and visitors. On hearing that she donates proceeds from her numerous worldwide speaking engagements to such causes as the education of Liberian children, one of her aides remarked, "She has the biggest heart I've ever known!" while another added, "She is very nice, but she is no push-over, believe me!"

Accustomed now to having her wishes obeyed, she can be impatient and sometimes overbearing with those who serve her. But at the same time she often displays surprising humility. For example, when Angie Brooks heard that she was to be honored by all the national chapters of Alpha Kappa Alpha, the black sorority that she joined at Shaw University, she asked, "But who else are you honoring?"

Her two sons, Wynston and Richard Henries, college-educated, are now well established in business and have provided her with grandchildren. But, remembering her own debt to the people who helped her, she has been foster mother to some forty-seven other Liberian boys and girls, raising them and putting them through school. Some of them live on a rubber plantation which she owns in Wearlah, fifty-five miles from Monrovia. Since Liberia has virtually no public welfare system, most needy children depend on the help of such private citizens. At least one of Angie Brooks's adopted children is now teaching in Liberia; another attended Shaw University. As a special assistant to the executive secretary of the American-founded Lott Carey Baptist Foreign Mission Convention, she has supervised a high school it sponsors in Liberia, as well as other projects.

Miss Brooks's original interest in law has never diminished; she has continued to work for the advancement of women in this profession, as well as for women's rights generally, through the United Nations and through the International Federation of Women Lawyers. From 1956 to 1959 she was Liberia's vice-president in the International Federation of Women Lawyers, representing both the federation and her country at the first session of the UN Economic Commission for

Africa. She also served two years as vice-president of the National Liberation Political and Social Movement. And she still serves as Liberia's assistant secretary of state.

Aside from her professional occupations, Angie Brooks's personal tastes and interests are wide-ranging. A large woman, she generally prefers colorful African garb for her public appearances, often making the long, flowing, matching *lappas* (skirts) and turbans herself. Her African art collection, including rare Benin bronzes, carved ivories, beaded works, and many ancient religious objects, is so large that a special museum has been built in Liberia to house it.

One of her favorite recreations is dancing and she has the reputation of being a charming hostess. People who know her speak of her warmth, humor, and vivacious manner. In spite of her exalted position and the elegance of her surroundings—when in New York she generally takes a suite at the Plaza—she is not above going into the kitchen herself to whip up a tasty dish.

Since the day she pestered President Tubman to send her to the States for a law education, many other women have followed in Angie Brooks's footsteps: Mrs. Justice Emma Shannon Walser was recently appointed by President Tubman's successor, President Tolbert, as Liberia's first woman judge, and Monrovia now has a woman mayor, Mrs. Ellen Sandimanie. Angie Brooks's influence continues to be felt not only in her own country but all over Africa, and, most of all, in the United Nations, in which she still holds unshakable faith. She has offered to go anywhere in the world where she might be of help in solving conflicts.

"The UN," she said in her inaugural speech as president, "could and should remain the best means of international cooperation that has been at mankind's disposal since the beginning of his history, and we have to nurse it and cherish it and cultivate it, or else we shall one day perish and not even the moon or the knowledge of space will save us."

SIERRA LEONE/ NIGERIA

Irene Ighodaro

Among the women doctors making their mark all over Africa one of the most distinguished is Dr. Irene Elizabeth Beatrice Ighodaro, a privately practicing physician and chairman of the board of management of the University of Benin Teaching Hospital in Benin City, Nigeria.

Mother of five, Dr. Ighodaro's accomplishments in the field of medicine are staggering: consultant in maternal and child health to the World Health Organization (WHO) since 1967 and just elected for another five-year term; author of *Baby's First Year*, a book published by Collins, Glasgow, Scotland, as well as many articles for magazines and newspapers; member and trustee of the Nigeria Medical Association; member of medical advisory committees in western Nigeria. In 1971 she received Nigeria's professional award,

F.M.C.G.P., establishing her as a Foundation Fellow, eligible to serve as consultant and examiner in her field.

Besides all this, she has held important national and international posts with the YWCA, with various church organizations, served on the boards of governors of many schools, and has been active in national and international associations of university women. In 1958 she received the civic award of M.B.E. (Member of the British Empire).

Though Dr. Ighodaro's career has been largely in Nigeria, where her husband is a judge of the High Court of Midwestern Nigeria, she was born and grew up in Sierra Leone, a small country on the upper west coast of Africa. In proportion to its population Sierra Leone has produced an impressively large number of doctors, including such eminent figures as Dr. John Karefa Smart, former associate director of the World Health Organization, Dr. "Charlie" Easmon, heading an outstanding medical family, and other women doctors, such as Dr. Dinah Jarrett, gynecologist and specialist in public health. Dr. Ighodaro's brother, Dr. Robert P. Wellesley-Cole, is a distinguished surgeon and author living in Freetown (capital of Sierra Leone), and her sister, Mrs. Taiwo Chariff, was formerly a nursing sister at the University College Hospital in Ibadan, Nigeria.

But neither Sierra Leone nor Nigeria can claim Dr. Ighodaro exclusively. In demand at conferences all over the world dealing with health, education, the family, women's causes, and church affairs, she has traveled extensively in every continent except South America; eleven and a half years of her life were spent in Britain which she still visits frequently, and since 1959, as a member of the YWCA World Executive Committee, based in Geneva, she has made annual trips to Switzerland.

For the fact that she has been able to do all this and still raise a family successfully Dr. Ighodaro gives much credit to her husband, Justice Samuel O. Ighodaro, who, she says, is "very broadminded and

Dr. Irene Ighodaro.

believes completely in the education of persons (male and female) and the continuous development of the personality. So I have great freedom of movement and action—with his help. Our goals are the same."

Actually Dr. Ighodaro has had strong family support all her life. It was her father, Wilfred S. Wellesley-Cole, a professional engineer, who encouraged her to become a doctor, and her doctor brother, Dr. Robert Wellesley-Cole, helped to finance her education.

Sierra Leone, like its neighbor Liberia, had once been a colony for ex-slaves, hence the name of its principal port and capital: Freetown. In 1787 it had been set up by the British Society for the Abolition of Slaves as a self-governing colony for freed slaves brought over from England—some of them freed in return for their helping the British fight the American Revolution—and also for others rescued from captured slave ships. The Africans thus brought together were of great diversity; uprooted from their families and traditions, many of them adopted British names and customs. After the British took over the colony in 1808 foreign domination increased, yet the Africans here remained more aggressive than elsewhere on the continent: e.g., the first black African university was established in Sierra Leone in 1844 and it was here that the first African nationalists of the Gold Coast and Nigeria were trained; newspapers started in Sierra Leone in 1855; it has been the birthplace of many prominent poets and composers. Sierra Leone became independent again in 1961.

So it was in this small but influential country that Irene Elizabeth Beatrice Wellesley-Cole was born, into a family of relative privilege. The house in which she grew up, along with four brothers (one died in infancy) and two sisters, was a three-storied reinforced concrete building halfway up the slope of Mount Aureol, Freetown. As she describes it:

There was a front verandah on each floor. The house commanded an excellent view of the estuary of the Sierra Leone River—we could see ships which came right into the mouth of the river and smaller ships and sailing boats and canoes going up and down the length of the river. We had magnificent view of sunrise and sunset. The house was situated in $3\frac{1}{2}$ acres of land on which fruits like mangoes, avocado pears, pawpaws, guavas, pineapples, etc. were grown.

In those days there was no servant problem. We, the children did the housework and cooking—on a wood cooking range. But all the heavy work, including chopping wood, was done by the servants.

My father was a water engineer, so we had our own dam and private water supply including complete irrigation for the farm. My mother was a keen gardener so with the help of the servants we had more than enough and to spare of every type of vegetable.

We kept a few chickens. We always had dogs and cats for pets and the boys had monkeys, and white mice from time to time.

Asked about what kind of clothes they wore, Dr. Ighodaro replied, "Alas, only Western type of clothes!" Her mother was a dressmaker. But some African customs did prevail:

Girls had their ears pierced for earrings when 7 days old and boys were circumcised on the 9th day of birth.

Those days—7th for girls and 9th for boys—were the Komojade Ceremony.* The priest (Christian) was called in to

* This Komojade Ceremony is similar to one in Ghana called "Outdooring."

pray for the baby, who was taken outside the house for the first
time, to show him to and from home to familiar places like
church, market, school and so on. At these ceremonies, food
like beans, plantains, potatoes—was always cooked in red palm
oil.

As a rule one went to neighborhood schools, but we went to
a government school which was supposed to be very good. It
was about three miles away. We walked there and back mostly
through short cuts by the side of the mountain.

After attending the Government Model School for her elementary
education, Irene Wellesley-Cole finished high school at the Annie
Walsh Memorial School, also in Freetown. Her decision to go into
medicine was prompted by some family circumstances:

It is strange. I was going to read Modern Languages, but
this was shelved for some time because my mother became seriously ill and I nursed her single-handed for three months. I
was the only daughter at home at the time.

After her death, my brother who had just qualified as a doctor, offered to pay for any course I chose to do and my father
suggested,

"Have you thought of Medicine? Why not do medicine?
You would be of use to many more people."

So I just agreed. But that meant I had to do Science. I had
never done Science before. . . . Luckily the University accepted Mathematics, Geography and Hygiene as Science and I
did French and Latin as foreign languages (English was not accepted as one). So I was accepted as a pre-medical student (at
the Medical School, King's College, University of Durham,
England) and had my first look down a microscope when I did

Botany in the pre-med class. So in my pre-medical year I had
to do Chemistry, Physics, Botany and Zoology—all brand new
subjects, but most fascinating!

No one was surprised when she emerged a full-fledged doctor with
an M.B.B.S. from Durham University, for all the Wellesley-Cole
children were talented and versatile. Besides Dr. Robert Wellesley-
Cole, already mentioned as a prominent surgeon and author, two
other brothers—Arthur and Eric—followed their father in the engineering profession. Arthur, who was also a lawyer, died in 1967. Eric
Wellesley-Cole is an inspector of plant machinery for the Sierra
Leone government. One sister, Winifred, married to Bishop P. Jones,
of Freetown, is a painter; the other, Mrs. Taiwo Chariff, has retired
from medical work and is now doing a full-time course in horticulture
in England.

Though still in frequent contact with her family and others in her
birthland, after her marriage to Samuel Ighodaro, Irene became more
closely associated with Nigeria. In fact many people today think she
was born and bred in Nigeria.

Justice Samuel Ighodaro and his wife have been extraordinarily
successful in merging two busy careers, raising and educating four
children (one died), and allowing everyone in the family complete
freedom and individuality. Before becoming judge of the high court
in midwestern Nigeria, Justice Ighodaro served as a tutor at Igbobi
College in Lagos (capital of Nigeria), minister of health of the Western Region, attorney general and minister of justice of the Western
Region, as well as senior lecturer at the University of Lagos. Two of
the three sons are already established in business: Anthony Onasero
Ighodaro is an engineer and businessman in London, while Wilfred
Osarogie, a mathematician, now works with Mobil Oil in Lagos. The
third son, Ayodele Osadebamwen, is studying physics at the Univer-

sity of Ibadan, northeast of Lagos. The only daughter, Oluyinka
Osayamwen, is at school also in Ibadan, preparing for the West African School Certificate Examination.

The Ighodaros have had to cope, as have so many modern-day Africans, with the changing views on women and the family. Not all the
people in either Sierra Leone or Nigeria have been as liberated in
their views as they. According to Dr. Irene Ighodaro, traditional
views of women have been "that they should do all the house work
and look after their husband and children. Those with initiative can
trade. If they live in the rural areas they help on the farm. The man is
the undisputed master, no nonsense."

But with the changing times, she says:

> People have now seen that it is true a woman changes her
> name after she is married, but a girl tends to have more filial
> affection than a boy, even after marriage. The tendency now is
> to encourage girls to acquire as much education as possible, but
> at the same time to keep her home together. There is now
> more discussion between marriage partners and more and
> more, marriage is becoming a partnership.

As to her own views on marriage, she says:

> It is the most demanding and most difficult career and yet it
> is rather difficult to prepare for it, for each is different.
> When both partners get on well—understand and like each
> other and enjoy a great deal of trust—it is wonderful. But if
> they don't it could be the worst hell.
> The pattern of marriage is undergoing changes, but I feel
> for an ordered society it is important that the institution of

Dr. Irene Ighodaro and family in garden of her home.

IDEAL STUDIO

marriage should be maintained. Society, I feel, is better for the discipline of marriage.

Because she and her husband agreed at the outset to share responsibilities, her own marriage has been the ideal partnership described above, e.g.:

As a professional woman with a home and career, I have two full time jobs for which good health is of the utmost importance. I accept it as my duty to see the good running of my home. Luckily I have a cooperative husband—but he cannot cook and he cannot sew buttons—a chore which was necessary when the children were small; but he could get up at night to attend to them, which he always did.

Being the wife of a prominent man, however, has added some special problems; it is not always practically possible to keep to the prestigious style of life commonly expected, e.g.:

In the fifties when my husband was Minister of Health, in Ibadan, early one morning, some staff from the Ministry of Information came to the house to do an interview and they were shocked to find this doctor, a medical woman and wife of a Minister, in the kitchen preparing breakfast (our domestic staff had gone) before beginning her day's professional work. They have never forgotten it!

Having children has interrupted her medical career at times, though never for very long.

Having five children created special problems, because although we doctors always tell our patients that pregnancy is physiological, I was never the physiological patient. This would have affected my practice badly if I did not work hard at it.

With my opportunities, if I had been a man, I would have been more mobile, but most times I travelled away from home I had to rush back to see to the welfare of the family.

Introduced by a young man recently as the "president of the Women's Liberation Movement" in her area, Dr. Ighodaro admits she is considered a staunch feminist. However, she says she has been "lucky in my male friends" and in general gets along quite well with men.

My male friends are very helpful and support me. They safeguard my medical practice as much as possible and are very appreciative of my efforts. They give me the feeling that they are proud of my achievements and forgive my failings.

But one must confess that for a woman in a man's profession all is not rosy. I have always been a private doctor which is far more demanding than working in an institution. Somehow some male colleagues resent this and there is no depth to which they would not sink in order to undermine my practice. For example: A male colleague who was asked to look after my practice for me when I was away having a baby, used to say to my patients, "Where is your doctor now?" and charge them exorbitantly.

One male doctor whom I begged to look after my retainer for me, transferred the whole firm to his books. And he was at that time my personal doctor! But these cannot be called friends.

But some male doctors have been very good—even going out at 2 A.M. to see my patients when called.

Sometimes patients and other people have shown deep prejudice:

Certain sections of this community are quite uncultivated and do not know to speak politely to a woman. In this connection I remember an old driver of ours whom I was reprimanding, saying to me, "I have two like you at home."

Another time, there was a serious accident right outside my clinic. The driver of the minibus had his foot rammed between the steering column and the seat. I explained to him in a cool, calm voice that I was a doctor; he was to remain quiet and calm and we would soon have his foot free. He looked up at me, just barely refraining from hissing, and continued tugging away till he got what he wanted—his body free and separated from the foot which remained trapped!

But Dr. Ighodaro feels, on the other hand, that women have some special advantages which men do not have:

> True, this is a man's world, but civilized men try to be courteous and chivalrous as long as the woman does not throw her weight around, does not ask for special favours and acts honestly and conscientiously. If one behaves politely, I find the men "go the extra mile" for one.

In spite of her busy practice and her worldwide commitments, Dr. Ighodaro has been generous in sharing her insights with a number of organizations dealing with home and family problems. She has served on the Ibadan Juvenile Court panel, the Ibadan Marriage Guidance Council, the Ibadan Diocesan Synod, as well as on the archbishop of West Africa's committee to study forms of marriage. She is a former national president of the Nigerian YWCA, and a past vice-president of the World YWCA. She also has been national president of the Nigerian Association of University Women and is currently a member of the Educational and Cultural Committee of the International Federation of University Women, as well as a trustee of the Nigerian Experiment in International Living.

Dr. Ighodaro's achievements in the field of medicine and service in so many other areas are all the more significant because she has been singled out, time and again, in a land of remarkable women. Nigeria has enjoyed an enviable reputation for some years for its large number of women leaders in every profession.

Yet Irene Ighodaro, like all great women, sees nothing remarkable in what she has done and is reluctant to talk about herself.

On other subjects she speaks freely; particularly interesting are her comments on some of the countries she has visited:

> America is wealthy and has a high general level of education. The women have a great deal of freedom and a great deal of leisure. "Neighborhood" and "brotherhood" have real meaning in America and that is responsible for a lot of the troubles.
>
> I am so used to England, I hardly consider it a foreign country, I criticize it as harshly as I criticize Nigeria and Sierra Leone.
>
> Japan is fantastic. . . . Thailand, beautiful; I wish I could understand more of the religions concept. . . . India, amazing.
>
> Senegal . . . the Haute Couture and elegance of the women is unforgettable.

Most telling is Dr. Ighodaro's comment on Rhodesia, a land rivaling South Africa in its oppression of black people:

> Rhodesia . . . a beautiful country "where every prospect pleases and only man is vile." The children do not laugh and play as in West Africa.

KENYA

Margaret Kenyatta

> I can remember the crowds of people who used to visit him
> at home, and I often used to make him play with me and he
> held me up in front of the people and they all laughed.*

Margaret Wambui Kenyatta was only a toddler at this time which
she recalls so vividly. It was 1930, and her father, Jomo Kenyatta, had
just returned to Kenya from a visit to England where he had gone to
present the grievances of the Kikuyu people against the British colonial government. White settlers had driven the Kikuyu from their
rich farming and pasture lands, forcing the Africans to live in reserva-
tions designated by the British government. Though it took well over
thirty years more—not until 1963—for Kenya to win independence,
the name of Kenyatta, meaning "Burning Spear," very soon became
one of the best known in Africa. For years people speculated about

* George Delf, *Jomo Kenyatta—Towards Truth About "The Light of Kenya,"* London, Victor
Gollancz Ltd., 1961, p. 74.

the man associated with the Mau Mau uprising, accused of plots with Moscow, constantly watched and finally jailed, idolized by some, feared and reviled by others. Today as president of Kenya, Mzee ("Elder") Jomo Kenyatta is one of the most venerated of African statesmen; children all over the world are named for him.

"Margaret Follows in Mzee's Footsteps" read the headline of a recent article in *Drum* magazine, showing pictures of the Kenya leader's eldest daughter taking the oath of office as mayor of Nairobi. The article goes on to say:

> She is calm and confident. She exudes an air of feminine charm but beneath her charm lies a toughness that is characteristic of her great father, Mzee Jomo Kenyatta.
> Margaret Wambui Kenyatta, the Mayor of Nairobi, has seen bitterness and strife in the struggle for Kenya's independence. But like her father, she has no room for bitterness in her heart. As Mayor of the cosmopolitan city of Nairobi, she serves people of all races, religions and tribes.*

Mrs. Ruth Njiiri, a friend long associated with the Kenyatta family, says of her:

> Margaret possesses a certain charisma with which her father is endowed. She looks very much like him and exudes a warmth that has enabled her to mingle with people of all stations. Her rise to Mayor of Nairobi (she is the first African woman mayor; there was previously a European woman mayor) was conscientiously worked on by Margaret without using her father's influence. She has always tried to remain in

* *Drum*, February, 1972.

the background and not accept special privileges because of her father.

Many people have expressed surprise that Wambui—as she is also known—has not taken advantage of political opportunities easily open to her. She is obviously her own woman.

City politics is not Miss Kenyatta's only interest. All her life has been devoted to nation-building and she has served wherever her remarkable talents could help: in political parties such as KANU (Kenya African National Union), the leading party today; in various women's organizations such as the YWCA, Girl Guides, and particularly the National Council of Women, of which she was president for three years; in the Kenya Red Cross; in various public health programs—she is a past chairman of the Public Health Committee; in business concerns—she is currently chairman of ALGAK, the Association of Local Government Employees; on school boards. Miss Kenyatta has also represented Kenya at the United Nations and been a member of various party and government delegations to African and other countries of the world. In 1964 Emperor Haile Selassie of Ethiopia decorated her with the Order of the Queen of Sheba.

While her distinguished and varied career is remarkable by any standards, it is even more noteworthy in the setting of her country at the particular time she grew up. Traditionally, women of East Africa were expected to marry, bear children, obey their husbands, and carry the main burden of domestic work and food raising. Single women were rare and the limited educational and job privileges available to Africans were generally reserved for men. Furthermore, East African women have had a reputation for being more conservative as a group than their West African sisters; e.g., the colorful, very independent market women so plentiful in Ghana and Nigeria were practically unknown in Kenya.

But Wambui defied tradition. Remaining single, with no formal education beyond high school, she nevertheless rose to a position of high esteem, commanding universal respect for her efficient handling of high-level discussions, both in Kenya and abroad; though she is modest, she is not timid.

Margaret Wambui was one of two children born to Jomo Kenyatta by his first wife, Nyokabi. The other child was a son named Peter Muigai. Kenyatta had three other wives, in succession: an English-woman by whom he had another son, also called Peter (Peter Magana), then a wife who died, leaving him a daughter, also named Wambui (Jane Wambui), and finally his present wife, Ngina, who has borne him four children.

Margaret Wambui Kenyatta was born at Nairobi, the capital of Kenya, in 1928. Her father left the following year for the first of several trips abroad, all of which were to have a profound influence on him and his country. He studied in both Russia and England, and in 1938 wrote a book, *Facing Mount Kenya*, which is still considered a classic in the anthropological field.

Margaret grew up in the Dagoretti area of Nairobi. She first attended the Ruthimitu Primary School, then went to the Church of Scotland Mission School at Kikuyu, and finally to the Alliance High School. She left the Alliance High School at the level of what is now called Form II, and went to teach at the Kenya Teachers College at Githunguri, where her father was principal. Githunguri College was a product of the Kikuyu Independent Schools Association, which had been formed in 1921 to give Africans opportunity to continue traditional practices not allowed in the missionary schools. Though he had been baptized as a Christian, Jomo Kenyatta saw no conflict—as some of the missionaries did—in his Christian and tribal beliefs. Furthermore, his experience abroad had convinced him that, as he put it, "the African—has a worthier essential way of life than the Euro-

Miss Margaret Kenyatta takes the oath of office as mayor of the city of Nairobi.

pean," and teachers at Githunguri College were trained and indoctrinated in this philosophy.

The British did not take such self-assertion seriously until Africans began to be more vocal and, finally, violent in their protests against white suppression. Though there were many conflicting reports about

Kenyatta's involvement with the Mau Mau and others causing the violence, because of his great popularity he was the most suspect. On October 21, 1952, the governor of Kenya declared a state of emergency and on the same day arrested Kenyatta and five of his associates. A few weeks later he closed the African Independent Schools because of "connection with Mau Mau."

Margaret Kenyatta had been teaching at Githunguri about four years when it was closed by this government order. During the emergency she, too, was arrested and detained for a week but was later released. She came back to Nairobi, and in order to keep alive, took various jobs as a telephone operator, with a bookbinding shop, and as a junior accounts clerk. During the period her father was on trial and later sentenced to prison for seven years, she became active in the Peoples Congress Party, a political party fighting for African rights and the release of political detainees. She also became deeply involved in many social welfare organizations dealing with women and general matters. One of the most important of Kenya's women organizations, Maendeleo ya Wanawake, was established in 1952.

In April, 1959, Jomo Kenyatta was released from jail, though his activities were restricted for a while longer. The protests of Africans had now grown so strong that the British government could no longer ignore them. The Kenya African National Union (KANU) was formed in 1960, to work for African liberation, and Jomo Kenyatta was made head of it. Margaret Wambui began working for the party as soon as it was formed; she was assistant secretary and later secretary of the KANU branch at Kiambu. She was also active in the Women's Wing of KANU, both at Kiambu and on the national level. During this period she became a county councillor at Kiambu.

A general election in May, 1963, resulted in an overwhelming victory for the KANU of Jomo Kenyatta; in December of the same year the British recognized the independence of Kenya and Mzee Jomo

Kenyatta became prime minister. The next year Kenya adopted a republic form of government with Kenyatta as president.

White settlers and the many other foreigners who had long lived
off the fat of the land now feared retaliation for their discrimination
against the Africans, and many began leaving. But they were surprised to find the new government not at all vindictive; in fact, all foreigners were given an opportunity to become full-fledged citizens of
Kenya.

Harambee—a Swahili word meaning "Pull together"—became the
watchword of the new regime, which emphasized that there would be
no racial, ethnic, class, or sexual domination. In his election-night address Prime Minister Kenyatta took special note of the women: "The
women of Kenya, too," he said, "will be given every encouragement
to involve themselves in the exciting task of Nation building."

His daughter, Margaret Wambui, echoed the challenge in an article which she wrote outlining some specific plans for women. The article, which received headlines, concluded with these words:

> So here is the great chance for which all we women have
> been waiting—or, at any rate, for which we ought to have
> been waiting. . . . This great crusade which the government is
> launching can bring new life to our community, in particular it
> can bring new life to the rural areas where the mass of our peo-
> ple live.*

The women of Kenya responded enthusiastically, for it seemed the
government was offering them exactly what they wanted. But it
wasn't all that easy to break patterns that had been set for many years.

They were disappointed, first of all, that not a single woman was

* Margaret Kenyatta, "Women and Harambee," *Pan Africa*, Feb. 21, 1964.

elected to the house of representatives; this was a step backward, for even under the colonial regime there had been two Kenyan women serving as appointed members of parliament. When some of the men suggested that women weren't interested in politics and should make their contributions in their homes and kitchens, there were furious protests. One woman signing herself "Wairimu" engaged in a newspaper debate on the subject:

> Even if it were a matter of kindness, there ought to have been a woman in the National Assembly. I wonder whether the public is aware that at the Kenya polls women, who are supposed to be socially subservient, outnumbered the men in the queues by three to two? In many reports received at the polling stations, the story was the same: "They waited hour after hour, shuffling slowly forward. Some waited and then had to return the next day."
>
> Among the pregnant women who gave birth as they waited, was one who delivered her child and then insisted on voting before being taken to hospital. She was so enthusiastic to vote!
>
> If the women of Kenya are to identify themselves with the task of Nation building and social reconstruction, then their voice should be heard. At the formation of the first true African Government in Kenya, the women should also have as much say as anybody else in the country.*

In spite of the disappointment of not having a woman representative in the new national government, some women were assuming important leadership roles at other levels. Mrs. Grace Onyango, who was later to become Kenya's first African woman mayor and eventu-

* *East African Standard*, June 14, 1965.

ally a member of parliament, was in 1963 elected chairman of the education committee of Kisumu, an important town of Kenya; the same
year Miss Margaret Kenyatta was elected a councillor for Dagoretti
in the city council of Nairobi and continued to be reelected for the
next four years.

It was obvious, however, that intensive efforts had to be made to
alert all the women of Kenya to their important role in nation-building. As Mrs. Phoebe Asiyo, superintendent of women's prisons,
stated:

> Women, like all human beings, need direction, but they
> need more; sympathy and understanding. Left to themselves,
> they will be as locusts in the nation's cornfields. But, if they are
> harnessed, treated with respect and given a fair share in all the
> fields, they present a great and powerful force which can be
> used for the benefit and progress of the Nation.*

For some years women had gathered in clubs and community cen-
ters all over the country. In the earlier years the activities of such organizations as the Maendeleo clubs centered more on homemaking
and home industries. But now there was more attention to advanced
education which would enable women to move more easily into commercial industry and government. It was no simple matter to get the
women together on what they wanted to achieve—there were petty
jealousies and some could think only in terms of themselves or their
tribes. But the broader-visioned women such as Margaret Kenyatta
patiently guided them to see what they could do through cooperation;
through contacts with international movements like Countrywomen
of the World, International Council of Women, Women Presbyteri-

* Celina Oloo and Virginia Cone, *Kenya Women Look Ahead*, Nairobi, Kenya, East African Literature Bureau, 1965, p. 40.

ans of Canada, and the YWCA, their thinking grew more unified. With help of funds from overseas the Kenya Council of Women was formed and ran some very successful seminars; in 1962 Miss Kenyatta was made chairman of the Kenya Women Seminar.

As a very small child Margaret Kenyatta's world had extended far beyond Kenya. First, as a part of the excited crowd gathered around her father each time he returned from a trip abroad, she stored information and impressions of countries she was later able to visit. Particularly after she became president of the National Council of Women of Kenya, in 1964, she began to travel widely, visiting countries in Europe, Asia, America, the U.S.S.R., and the People's Republic of China. When she attended the All-India Women's Conference in New Delhi she was the house guest of the then Prime Minister Nehru and his daughter, Mrs. Indira Gandhi, who later succeeded him. The people of India were much impressed with Miss Kenyatta, noting that she "radiated the quiet confidence and zeal of the new Africa to foster and build on its newly-won freedom."

In June, 1964, she was awarded the title of Officer of the Order of the Queen of Sheba by the emperor of Ethiopia.

Miss Kenyatta represented the National Council of Women of Kenya in many conferences and seminars overseas, including addresses to students in Washington, a seminar of women's leaders in Israel, various women's conferences in England, and elsewhere.

In October, 1965, Miss Kenyatta attended the 20th Session of the United Nations General Assembly and addressed the UN committee dealing with racial discrimination and fundamental human rights.

Closely connected with her championship of the rights of women has been Miss Kenyatta's deep interest in the education and well-being of children. A Nairobi newspaper article, reviewing her achievements, stated:

Rarely has she spoken on the subject of women taking active

part in life without also cautioning them in first attending to their own homes and children.

This, in Miss Kenyatta's opinion, is the first duty of every woman. For a happy, well-cared-for home serves nation-building. In today's children lies the hope for the future of Kenya, and Miss Kenyatta expressed this when she was guest of honor at a school in Nairobi. . . .

Kenya schools, she said, were the only place where children of different races and religions had the chance of mixing and working together.*

Today, with all her other duties, Miss Kenyatta finds time to serve on the boards of governors of a number of secondary schools.

Margaret Kenyatta has also been active for a long time in the field of public health. As a member of the Nairobi City Council she played a prominent role in the administration of public health. She was chairman of Pumwani Maternity Hospital Sub-Committee during the reconstruction and extension of the hospital and also served as chairman of the Public Health Committee.

When some seats in parliament became vacant in May, 1966, everyone expected Margaret Kenyatta to enter the election contest. Her prospects for becoming Kenya's first woman legislator seemed good, for she had easily won her seat in the Nairobi City Council three years before, decisively defeating some strong male opponents. But she announced she would not run. While declining this opportunity for herself, she emphasized once again her belief that women should advance in politics.

"In this country," she said, "there should be no discrimination between men and women; they should be judged only by their abilities."

* *East African Standard*, August 20, 1969.

In her addresses to women's groups she said that women had lagged behind because they were deprived of their privileges, but it was now up to the women themselves to find a way to participate actively in nation-building. Women listened to Miss Kenyatta because they knew she spoke from personal experience. Readily conceding that it was not easy being a woman in a man's world, she said, "You must be prepared for disappointment—you don't win all the time; more often you lose even when all the odds seem to be in your favor."

Miss Margaret Kenyatta, mayor of Nairobi, greets President Mzee Jomo Kenyatta on his way to Uhuru Park.

MERAPIX, NAIROBI, KENYA

Later, reflecting on her over four years as a city councillor, she said, "I am always learning. It is hard work and you can never know it all."

In July, 1969, Miss Margaret Kenyatta was elected deputy mayor of Nairobi; in 1971 she was unanimously elected mayor, for a two-year term. Thus she became the first African woman to become mayor of Kenya's capital and the second African woman mayor of Kenya. (Mrs. Grace Onyango, mayor of Kisumu, was the first.)

As mayor of Nairobi Miss Kenyatta has had to make some unpopular decisions, but she never swerves from her convictions. Among the many development programs announced since she took office have been some plans for building of traffic fly-overs, subways, and underground stations in Nairobi—all to be completed by the turn of the century—as well as massive outlays of capital for low-cost housing and sewerage.

Margaret Wambui Kenyatta is a familiar figure as she moves about into the life of the city and country. Like her father she is a skillful orator, but she also knows how to listen. A recent photo showed her talking to a group of elderly men, indicating her awareness of the older people with their store of African traditional values.

Apart from politics, Miss Kenyatta is "becoming quite an astute business woman," says a friend. As current chairman of ALGAK—the Association of Local Government Employees—she heads an organization that is overwhelmingly masculine, but she handles it, as she does everything else, with confidence and authority.

"What is the secret behind her success? Is it hereditary?" asked *Drum* magazine in its article of February, 1972. "This is a difficult question to tackle but Margaret believes in thorough planning and homework."

Miss Kenyatta, described by one person who has known her a long time as "nowadays a mature woman with large sad eyes and a rare but

President Jomo Kenyatta of Kenya, father of Margaret Kenyatta.

infectious laugh," is available to her people but shuns interviews with press or anyone seeking to publicize her personal story.

Whatever explains her success, everyone who has met her, or felt her influence nationally and internationally, would agree with this comment of Mrs. Njiiri:

> She is definitely, though quietly, showing Kenyan males that an unmarried woman can play an effective role in the society. Although she is not one to be ashamed of her simple rural home and environment, she does believe in upward mobility. There is no doubt in my mind that she will continue to be a forerunner in the women's quest for liberation and inclusion in the decision-making positions in government and private industry.

ZAMBIA

Gwendoline Konie

Among the conferences on women's rights that have been held in Africa in growing numbers through the past ten or fifteen years, one which took place in Zambia in late November, 1970, was particularly significant. As a reporter described it, this was "no frivolous 'women's lib' rally but a solemn assembly of Zambian women examining their rights in the areas of marriage, divorce and widowhood under both customary (tribal) law and statutory law." *

According to the same reporter, a journalist by the name of Omar Eby, he and a professor of law were the only men allowed to attend the conference and only because each had specific duties to perform. While the professor had some papers to read, Mr. Eby's job was to act as a sort of buffer between the supposedly "shy" women and aggres-

* Omar Eby, "Zambian Women Recommend Reform in Marriage Laws," *Christian Century*, September 22, 1971.

sive press members who might try to interview them. But the journalist soon found himself out of work. As he put it, "the conferees—some 50 vocal and argumentative women—proved to need no such protection. At the consultation's fiasco of a press conference the gentlemen of the press became downright timid in the presence of the ladies, then went away and fabricated their own innocuous versions of the affair." *

The person who *was* able to handle this lively group—which included such notables as Mrs. Betty Kaunda, wife of the president, and other women, less literate, speaking only African dialects—was its young chairman, Miss Gwendoline Chomba Konie. The report issued after the meeting expressed particular gratitude to Miss Konie, noting that it was she who, "through her own confidence and natural charm, created a cordial, yet business-like, atmosphere. She played a dual role as vernacular interpreter as well and bridged potential gaps in the difficult post-consultation task of interpreting the recommendations to the press, radio, and television." ** The report went on to express gratitude for Miss Konie's "articulate explanations and her personal commitment to the cause of women's rights."

Highest-ranking woman in the Zambian civil service, now working toward a law degree, Gwendoline Konie—still only in her early thirties—has distinguished herself in a number of fields: as a professional social worker, member of the first legislative council of her country in which Africans were represented, UN delegate for three years, head of the African desk for Zambia, and deputy commissioner for Zambia at the 1970 Japan World Exposition. There are other fields in which she could have had a career if she wanted: She is an accomplished singer and actress, winning the best actress award in the 1966 Drama

* *Ibid.*

** *Women's Rights in Zambia*, Mindolo Ecumenical Foundation, Kitwe, Zambia, Foreword.

Miss Gwen Konie, UN delegate from Zambia, looks on while P. Dapcevic (Yugoslavia) addresses the meeting.

Festival run by the Theatre Association of Zambia. In addition she has served on many important governing boards—before independence when Zambia was still called Northern Rhodesia, she was on the board of the Northern Rhodesia Broadcasting Corporation; among those on which she serves today are the Hotel's Board of Zambia, the Lusaka YWCA Executive, the Adult Education Association of Zambia, and the Family Planning Association.

For a young black woman to achieve all this and make such significant contributions to her country, before she is thirty-five, is no easy matter, even if she is beautiful and brilliant. Women in Zambia are still victims of discrimination in many ways—as the consultation clearly showed—and it is only within the last ten years that Africans here have begun to firmly shake off the shackles of apartheid, the white supremacy policy that has made life so intolerable for their neighbors to the south, in Rhodesia and South Africa.

Like others in this book, Gwen Konie gives her parents credit for her achievement. Born at Lusaka—capital of the country—on October 9, 1938, Gwendoline Chomba Konie grew up, with four brothers and five sisters, in a home that stressed education and hard work. Both parents were teachers. William Bernard Chinyimba Konie, her father, was a great liberal for his time, believing in education for both girls and boys. Describing him, Miss Konie says:

> Father was quiet spoken, deliberate and slow to anger and demanded obedience with the use of only one or two words. He had a scientific mind and could never understand it when any of his children found it difficult to do arithmetic and mathematics. It was not unusual to find him browsing through an algebra or geometry book for relaxation. He put great store on education and sent all the children to boarding school at an early age. There were always at least three Konie children in boarding school at a time. This must have been quite a feat since African salaries at the time were very poor indeed. Father was a Headmaster of one school or another ever since I was old enough to remember such a detail. He worked in ten

different areas all together and died in 1960, two years after re-
tirement, rather prematurely . . . probably because he had
worked too hard throughout his life.

Miss Konie's mother, Hilda Kalulu Konie, began also as a professional
teacher, but today she is in charge of the Nurses' Home at the Ronald
Ross Nurses' Training School, Mufulira Copper Mine. Mrs. Konie
ruled the children in a different way, being, according to her daughter, "an exacting woman in her demands and fastidiously clean, a
characteristic which I did not appreciate in my early years but which,
nevertheless, rubbed on to all the children; we are better for it, though
no one comes anywhere near Mother."

When she was nine years old Gwen Konie began attending Chipembi Girls' School, a boarding school run by Methodist missionaries.
At the time it was only a primary school, but a few years later it became a secondary school. For many years it was the only secondary
school for girls in the country, and competition for entry there was
stiff. Many of the outstanding women in the country were produced
at Chipembi. In December, 1957, Gwen Konie was one of the first
eight girls in the country ever to sit for the Cambridge School Certificate, an extremely difficult examination. Only one of the girls
failed, two got first-class division, and the rest, including Miss Konie,
achieved second division. This was a credit both to the staff of Chipembi School and to the quality of their students.

There had never been any doubt in Gwen Konie's mind that she
would go on to complete a university education. At one time she
thought of becoming a doctor, but gave it up when she realized her
lack of preparation; since there were no laboratories at Chipembi it
could not offer any science courses other than math. She also toyed
with the idea of studying music, but her father frowned on this. Finally she was attracted to some short courses for social workers, being

given by a former British officer then working in the country. Gwen Konie did so well in this that she won a federal scholarship to do social science at a university in England. From 1959 until September, 1961, she studied at University College of Swansea in Wales, where she took a diploma in social science. Except for the sadness caused by her father's death in February, 1960, it was a happy time; she participated fully in the university life, both academically and socially: she was a member of the university choir, the fencing club, the athletic club. She also took a great interest in the Labour party activities, mainly because of the party's liberal policy toward decolonization.

At this time, in the early 60's, Northern Rhodesia was caught up in the move for independence that had spread all over the continent. Inspired by Ghana, which had achieved independence in 1957, one African nation after another was removing itself from colonial rule. The situation in Northern Rhodesia had been complicated because it had been forced to join a white-created federation with two other countries under British rule: Southern Rhodesia and Nyasaland (now Rhodesia and Malawi). Because of differences in leadership in the three countries it was difficult for Africans to organize in a common struggle against white domination. The apartheid—i.e., white supremacy—policies of South Africa had spread north; even though the British government of Northern Rhodesia was less exacting in its separation of black and white, African citizens there—in spite of their majority—had no real choice about where they could live, eat, or work. The free social life Gwen Konie led in Wales was impossible in her own country. Grown black men were called "boys" and allowed only at the back door—if at all—of places frequented by whites. But there were some black leaders in Northern Rhodesia who, in spite of frequent jailings for daring to oppose the system, had managed to pull African people together to demand an end to such discrimination.

The most outstanding African spokesman was a former school-teacher, Kenneth Kaunda, a deeply compassionate man strongly influenced by the nonviolent methods of Mahatma Gandhi. Under Kaunda's guidance Africans began to hope and work for delivery from their oppressed state. Fearful of his growing influence, the colonial government jailed him several times, accusing him of insurrection; but by the end of 1959, when he had again spent some months in jail, neither Kaunda nor his African followers could be ignored. On his release from jail in January, 1960, Kaunda declared his determination to achieve self-government for Africans in Northern Rhodesia; soon afterward he formed the United National Independence party (UNIP), which is the ruling party in Zambia today. The African name, "Zambia," taken from the Zambezi River, began to be used more and more instead of "Rhodesia," a name derived from the British explorer, Cecil Rhodes. As the movement for independence grew stronger, every African man, woman, and child began shouting, "Za-za-Zambia!" Another common watchword was "Kwacha!" which means "the dawn" (of independence). "Kwacha" is today the name of the Zambia currency.

When Gwen Konie came back home, in September, 1961, equipped with a diploma in social science, she found many changes, but the country still had far to go in granting Africans equality with whites. Her first job, doing probation work in the Ministry of Local Government and Social Welfare, gave proof of this. In spite of her high qualifications Miss Konie was given neither the title nor the salary to which she was entitled, that of assistant social welfare officer. In contrast, a white girl who had just come back from Salisbury University (in Southern Rhodesia) with a degree in French was immediately employed as an assistant social welfare officer. Many Africans might have resigned themselves to this situation, but not Gwendoline Konie. Here, in her own words, is what happened next:

Being young and hot headed, this treatment made me quite stubborn. I quarreled with my white colleagues, my supervisors and finally with the Colonial Chief Establishment Officer in the Civil Service. This final quarrel led to a reversal of the decision regarding my appointment. I was to become an Assistant Social Welfare Officer and got quite a handsome back pay.

This did not make me popular one bit. Therefore when one day I received a note from the Chief Secretary's office saying that he wanted to see me, I was convinced that the summons must mean that I was going to be sacked and, as a matter of fact, my colleagues thought so too. Unfortunately for me, my appointment fell at the time the Chief Secretary, Sir Richard Luyt, was acting as Governor because the Governor, Sir Evelyn Hone, was out of the country. This made me more nervous, but I was determined not to show my nervousness. To my surprise, instead of the Acting Governor dressing me down, he asked me about my background and more or less praised my performance. He then asked me whether I would accept a nomination into the Legislative Council. I asked for time to think the matter over.

I felt obliged to discuss the matter with Dr. Kenneth Kaunda in his capacity as leader of UNIP and government benches. This was a coalition government. He advised me to accept the nomination and on 2nd March, 1963, the Acting Governor, Sir Richard Luyt, nominated me to the Legislative Council. I was then 23, going on 24. . . .

The "coalition government" referred to by Miss Konie was the result of an election in late 1962 when African representatives were allowed to vote for the first time. Although the election was controlled by the colonial government, it did succeed in passing political power from European to African hands. Kenneth Kaunda's UNIP party received 60 percent of the vote but was forced to join in a coalition with the minority African party, ANC (African National Congress—not to be confused with the South African ANC); the European party, UFP (United Federal party), formed the opposition. Fifteen months later, in January, 1964, there was a general election in which everyone was allowed to vote, and this resulted in the selection of Kenneth Kaunda as prime minister. On October 24 of the same year, 1964, Northern Rhodesia became the independent Republic of Zambia and Kenneth Kaunda its first president.

From the time of her nomination to the Northern Rhodesia Legislative Council in 1963 up to the present, Gwendoline Konie has remained in government service, in various capacities. When parliament was dissolved at the end of 1963 in preparation for the Independence elections, Dr. Kaunda invited her to join others who had been chosen to train for the foreign service and she accepted.

From January to June, 1964, she trained, along with nine men from Northern Rhodesia, at the American University in Washington, D.C., where she received a certificate in international relations. To fulfill a requirement for practical experience, the U.S. State Department arranged for her to work for some weeks (June 29–August 9) in the British consul general's office in Los Angeles. For the rest of August until they got back to Northern Rhodesia the first week in September, 1964, Gwen Konie and her nine countrymen visited and studied a number of organizations, including the British Mission to the United Nations in New York, the British High Commission in Ottawa, Canada, and the British foreign service headquarters in London. Back in Lusaka, from September 14 through October 10, Miss Konie attended a seminar on foreign service run by the Dag Hammarskjold Foundation. The thirty particpants in this seminar came from the' then Northern Rhodesia, Malawi, Tanzania, Kenya, and

The Minister of Trade, the Hon. Mulemba, to the right of Miss Gwen Konie, is honored on Zambia National Day.

Uganda, and included three girls. The other two girl participants, besides Miss Konie, were both from Kenya.

At the end of the seminar at Lusaka, just two weeks before Independence, Gwendoline Konie and her nine male colleagues were attached to Prime Minister Kaunda's office. On Independence Day, October 24, 1964, this became the Ministry of Foreign Affairs.

Miss Konie's first foreign service assignment was on the United

Nations desk. She attended the 19th, 20th, and 21st sessions of the
United Nations in New York and sat on the Special Political Committee of the UN where she felt the experience gained "was tremendous."

In 1967 she moved on to African Affairs and was responsible for
the African Desk. From that year to 1969 she attended all meetings of
the Council of Foreign Ministers and those of the heads of state of the
OAU (Organization of African Unity, the organization of all the independent countries of Africa). With the exception of the August,
1968, meeting in Algiers, all meetings were held in the OAU headquarters in Addis Ababa, Ethiopia. As head of the African Desk, Miss
Konie traveled as the most senior officer from the Ministry of Foreign
Affairs. In 1968 she also attended the Commonwealth Heads of State
and Government Conference in London, which dealt with the controversial issue of Rhodesia, the country formerly called Southern
Rhodesia. Unlike its former associates in the federation, Northern
Rhodesia (Zambia) and Nyasaland (Malawi), which had achieved independence under black majority rule, Southern Rhodesia's white minority refused to let go of government control; though Britain refused
to grant independence under these conditions, the self-imposed white
minority government of Prime Minister Ian Smith defiantly pro-
claimed itself the independent Republic of Rhodesia in November,
1965. Worldwide debate about this illegal government has gone on
ever since.

At the time of the Japan World Exposition in 1970, Miss Konie
was assigned to the Ministry of Trade for the duration of the Exposition. She was nominated the deputy commissioner general for Zambia
at the Exposition in Osaka, Japan, and actually ended up doing the
commissioner general's work (since the commissioner general was
not resident in Japan). As she described it, this was "a tough assignment but rich in experience. . . . One had to be on one's toes all the
time," working for "something like twelve hours a day." Especially

Miss Gwen Konie with important guests at the Zambia Pavilion at Expo '70, Osaka, Japan.

demanding was the organization for Zambia's national day, with thousands of guests to cater for. But once again Gwendoline Konie distinguished herself and her country.

Among the many volunteer organizations with which Miss Konie has been associated, the Young Women's Christian Association has been one to which she has been particularly deeply committed. She joined the YWCA when it first came to Zambia, was president of the Lusaka branch twice, and then served as president of the National

YWCA for two years running. She is currently on the executive
board of the YWCA in the capital (Lusaka).

As a member of a committee investigating the need for establishing
a University of Zambia, Miss Konie contributed to the Lockwood Report, which recommended the establishment of such a university.

Although she has little time these days for nonprofessional activities, Gwen Konie has always had a deep interest in music and the theater, distinguishing herself as a singer and actress. In 1966 she won
the best actress award for her role in *Dear Parent and Ogre*, the Wad-
dington Theater's entry in the annual drama festival run by the Theater Association of Zambia. In music and in literature her tastes run
from light to serious.

Gwen Konie's interest in the status of women began long before
she chaired the consultation in Zambia in 1970. In 1963 she attended
the ECA (Economic Commission for Africa) Conference on the
"Role of Women in Urban Development" which was held in Lagos,
Nigeria. Interest in women's rights in Africa had been growing
through the years. Though in many ways African women have been
far ahead of their European and American sisters in achieving political
emancipation, generally (not always) on an equal footing with men
after their countries became independent, there are still traditional
customs and laws—especially some having to do with marriage and
property ownership—which have held them back in other respects.
Regional conferences held in Ethiopia (1960), Togo (1964), and
Ghana (1968) awakened women leaders of many countries; the UN
Declaration on the Elimination of Discrimination Against Women
(which Annie Jiagge helped formulate) was a further impetus.

Requests for the Consultation on the Rights of Women in Zambia
came from churches, women's political and professional organizations,
and many other people who felt the need for educating the women in
the country about their rights and for bringing the voice of women to
government in one body. The group of fifty women who assembled

in November, 1970, at the Mindolo Ecumenical Center near Kitwe stood for no nonsense and got right down to business. Sensing the alarm of Zambia's men, Mrs. Betty Kaunda, wife of the president, addressed her opening remarks to them, reassuringly but firmly:

> We are not seeking to overthrow tradition. . . . On the contrary, this consultation is concerned with the preservation of traditional values. It is the mother in the home who teaches the children about their heritage. . . . On the other hand, we recognize certain traditional practices which are no longer appropriate. . . . We (women) do not want to take away your authority and power. We talk about "woman power" but we do not mean it as a threat to "man power." We do not want to replace you men; we are in search of a role which will support and supplement your efforts.*

She then cautioned the women against regarding themselves as second-class human beings:

> We must not be bullied into apathy, into not caring and doing nothing.**

From there, under the skillful guidance of the petite chairman, Miss Gwendoline Konie, the conference got down to a discussion of women's rights, concentrating particularly on the changing patterns of marriage, and the confusion caused by Zambia's two legal systems: customary (tribal) law and statutory law (adapted from the British). At the end of the consultation, which lasted from November 20 to 24, 1970, the women drew up a summary statement and recommendations:

* Women's Rights in Zambia, pp. 9–13.

** *Ibid.*

We . . . accept the challenge of Mrs. Betty Kaunda to "unite our talents and energies to work towards stabilizing the position of women in our society." . . .

We acknowledge the rights enshrined in the Constitution of Zambia, yet are aware of the weaknesses in our legal system. We recognize that our country is passing through a period of rapid social change which has brought insecurity in family life and sexual ethics.

There were six main recommendations, with details spelled out under each. The first three dealt with establishing unified laws, i.e.,

1) a unified marriage law
2) a unified divorce law
3) a unified law of succession and inheritance

All of these were to be "based on provisions from both customary and statutory law which are appropriate to the present social situation in Zambia." The other recommendations were:

4) reform in laws regarding child support
5) move toward making polygamous marriage illegal
6) greater government concern for the rights of women

An incident occurring in Zambia shortly after this consultation pointed up the need for the recommended legislation: A husband and father of five children, employed in a supervisory job, decided to take a new wife. He sent away his first wife with only the clothes on her back, refusing to let her take even her youngest child, a two-year-old, with her. In spite of her anguished pleas he insisted the house, the children, furniture, and all the dishes belonged to him alone; he immediately installed the new woman as his wife, turning everything over to her.

Gwendoline Konie's contribution to the effectiveness of the consultation and implementation of its recommendations lasted far beyond the close of the meeting on November 24, 1970. Assuming a large share of the interpretation and dissemination of information from the meeting, she has continued up to the present to work for the advancement of women's rights. Here is what she feels about it:

The most far reaching changes in the status of women are to be found in post-independence Zambia. Women are in increasing numbers breaking away from kinship groups and striking out on their own, assuming responsibility for their own maintenance and that of their children. Nevertheless, at the moment, (due to inadequate facilities for girls' education in pre-independence Zambia) there are not many women who are able to find gainful employment whether it be in rural areas or in towns.

Post-independence Zambia has seen large scale liberalization of education. There are now no sex barriers in the educational system and it is the country's greatest hope that the near future will see as many professionally qualified women as men.

With this great awareness of the need for equal opportunities to education has arisen an equally great awareness amongst the women for self emancipation. The women are aware that although they have the same political rights as men, they are not so well off where social, family and inheritance laws are concerned. The Zambian woman is quite aware of the fact that the heights to which her status will climb will greatly depend on her own performance. She is further aware of the fact that, if she has to compete with men on equal basis, she has to push her present rate of performance all round.

It is hard to imagine how Gwendoline Chomba Konie could push her own "present performance rate" any higher, but apparently she plans to do so. In her spare time she is working toward a law degree with London University.

MADAGASCAR

Rahantavololona Andriamanjato

Rahantavololona Andriamanjato, first woman engineer in Africa, has almost as many jobs as she has names: wife of the mayor of Tananarive, capital of Madagascar (also called Malagasy); joint leader of AKFM (Party of Congress for the Independence of Madagascar), the opposition party; engineer of public works and chief of the water division of the Bureau of Mines and Energy; lay preacher assistant to her husband, who is also pastor of a large church in Tananarive. Mother of four children, the first lady of Tananarive is also active in organizations outside her country. Graciously responding to a letter soliciting more details about her life, she found time to handwrite a reply while en route to a meeting of the FDIP (International Democratic Federation of Women) in Bulgaria; from there she was going on to a conference in Cyprus sponsored by SODEPAX, a peace organization co-sponsored by the World Council of Churches and the Vatican.

Most people outside Madagascar, with the possible exception of the Welsh, have a lot of trouble pronouncing, not to mention spelling, the long Malagasy names. But in Africa, as everyone knows, all names—long or short—have meaning.

"I have a very long name," Mrs. Andriamanjato admits:

Rahantavololona Razanamahandry Alphonsine Razafindrako-tohasina Andriamanjato. Andriamanjato is the name of my husband, Razafindrakotohasina that of my father. It has been the family name since around 1939 when my father resigned himself to becoming a French citizen, so that we children could go to the Lycées which were exclusively reserved for the French people and French citizens. I say "resigned himself" because, truly, being so strongly a nationalist, he did this with death in his soul; on the other hand he thought that for the future of the country he had to make a sacrifice and thus be able to give a solid education to his children.

My names are actually the following feminine ones: Rahan-tavololona Razanamahandry Alphonsine.

Alphonsine is a French forename. Our parishioners call me Ramatoa Rahantavololona (Madame Rahantavololona) because the Malagasy, who have kept the ancestral traditions, do not approve of giving a man's name to a woman (such as the name of my father or of my husband). They prefer giving feminine names to women and masculine names to men.

Now I like to be called by the name Rahantavololona—"the one who is petted," or "who likes to be spoiled"—But perhaps when I pass the age of being petted, I will have to resign myself to bearing my other name, Razanamahandry, "she who is patient."

We can change names here like that.*

   Rahantavololona Razanamahandry Alphonsine Razafindrakotohasina Andriamanjato, whom for practical purposes we will hereafter
call Mrs. Andriamanjato, lives on one of the largest islands in the
world, with a uniquely romantic history. Known to navigators since
the fifteenth century, Madagascar, situated in the Indian Ocean near
the southeast tip of Africa, was once a favorite place for pirates.
Today because of its strategic location along the oil tanker routes
from the Middle East, what happens there is important to everybody.
   The people come from a diversity of backgrounds, the majority of
them with mixtures of Malaysian-Indonesian-Polynesian blood, including a group called the Merina; there are also people of Arabic
origin such as the Tsimihety, and some of African descent, the Bantu.
In spite of this great variety, however, all the people speak Malagasy,
a language with strong Oriental influence, as well as French, and
there is a distinctive style in their culture, combining African, Arabic,
and Oriental elements.
   Tananarive is situated in a high plateau region of the island, on the
site of the old capital city of the Merina kingdom. The Merinas, or
Hovas, people of Indonesian and Malaysian descent who came to
Madagascar during the first century, have been the traditional rulers,
their queens long known as the "Queens of Madagascar." Although
the whole island became a French protectorate in 1885, Merina have
resisted French rule, often breaking into bloody revolt. When, after
long agitation for constitutional reform, the French set up the Malagasy Republic in 1958, the provisional African government was
headed by Philibert Tsiranana, a Catholic of peasant stock (Tsimihety) whose political followers, the PSD (Social Democratic party),

* Translated from a letter written in French by Mrs. Andriamanjato.

TANANARIVE, MADAGASCAR

Mrs. Rahantavololona Andriamanjato.

were considered more moderate and favorable to the French. Tsiranana was later elected president of the Malagasy Republic, which became fully independent in 1960. Richard Andriamanjato, a Hova
(Merina) and Protestant, was elected at the same time (1959) as
mayor of the capital, Tananarive. Andriamanjato was the popular
leader of the opposition party AKFM (Malagasy Independence Congress party), considered more radical—or at least less pro-French.
Though the Merina, main supporters of AKFM in Tananarive, are
not in power today, they are considered the intellectual elite of the
country and wield a good deal of influence.

Marriage to a leader of the Merina aristocracy did not change
Rahantavololona Razafindrakotohasina's life too much, for she was
herself of the same background. When asked about people who have
most influenced her life, Mrs. Andriamanjato says without hesitation,
"My father and my husband."

Her father, a medical doctor in Tananarive, had twelve children,
ten of them girls. When his neighbors rather mockingly sympathized
with him for having the bad luck to get so many daughters—sons
would have been much more useful, they said—the doctor vowed that
his daughters would achieve as much as any men.

So he pressed his daughters to learn all they could. As already mentioned, he became a French citizen—even though it broke his heart—
in order to give his children the best education possible. When his
wife died in 1947 he could not afford a housekeeper, but he did not
break his vow. Dr. Razafindrakotohasina himself kept the house and
did all the cooking while his daughters continued going to school.

When the doctor died in 1957 most of his children were still
studying, but today his vow has been fulfilled: Two of his daughters
are doctors, two are librarians, one is an archaeologist, one a lawyer,
one an administrator, one an engineer, and one is a teacher. One who
is still in school hopes to also become a doctor.

Rahantavololona Razafindrakotohasina studied engineering in Paris, at the Women's Polytechnic School and then at the Sorbonne, where she specialized in applied aerodynamics, used in the design of airplanes. She wanted to study aircraft design, a rather unusual ambition for a Malagasy girl, but not so uncommon in Paris, as she pointed out:

> The Women's Polytechnic was famous for training aircraft designers. The Caravelle airliner was designed by women . . . former students of the school.*

But when she came back to Madagascar in 1959 with her certificate in Applied Aerodynamics, there was only one job available, that of Water Engineer. So she took it.

Now as Chief of the Water Division for Madagascar, Mrs. Andriamanjato is responsible for supplying water to 7 million people; she also teaches hydraulics to public works students at the University of Tananarive, a university with well over two thousand students.

As the first woman engineer, it was hard in the beginning for her to get men to take her seriously. "I had to be very good at my work," she says, "to show I was capable."**

But once they accepted her there was no problem and today everywhere she goes men and women alike express admiration for her work. In fact, she has encouraged many other women to enter the field and there are now no less than forty Malagasy women engineers.

Mrs. Andriamanjato's political and church life is very much intertwined with that of her husband, the remarkable mayor of Tanana-

---

* Quotation from interview with Mrs. Andriamanjato, *Africa Acts* Feature Service, Nairobi, Kenya, "The First Lady of Tananarive."

** *Ibid.*

rive, pastor of a large church, deputy of the national assembly, and president of AKFM. He, too, has worldwide commitments: vice-president of the Christian Conference for Peace (Prague), president of the All Africa Conference of Churches (based in Nairobi), and member of the presidium of the World Council on Peace (Helsinki); he has a reputation for being one of the most dynamic speakers anywhere.

Together the Andriamanjatos are a handsome, articulate pair, but it is not always possible for them to work as a team. When they were both elected in 1959 to the Tananarive Municipal Council, Richard Andriamanjato was made mayor and his wife was one of ten vice-mayors. However, in 1961, after Independence, a rule was made against married couples serving together on the council, so she left it. She does continue to share in the leadership of AKFM, the opposition party, being president of the largest local branch, in Tananarive itself; AKFM controls the city government here.

The church where her husband is pastor, Ambohitantely ("the mountain of honey"), is in the highest part of the city. Mrs. Andriamanjato often leads women's groups there during the weekend or goes to other churches to give what she calls "not exactly sermons, but little talks."

"I spend my day in the office, my evenings in politics and my week-ends in churches," she says. "Twenty-four hours in a day are not enough to do all I have to do."

Added to this are the many calls on her time outside the country. She and her husband both regret the frequent absence from their four children, ranging in age from six to eleven, and often wish they could enjoy more time at home. But they both believe passionately that the gifts God has given them cannot be spent on family alone and they feel a deep commitment to the world community. Her travels to conferences of women's groups, church and peace organizations, have carried her to many countries of Africa, Europe, and Asia. Aside from making her own contributions, Mrs. Andriamanjato has found many of these experiences personally enriching. Of all the interesting people she has met in her travels, one she admires most is the Soviet woman cosmonaut, Valentina Tereshkova:

> I met her for the first time in Moscow in 1963 after her space flight, and then afterwards at meetings of the FDIF (Democratic International Federation of Women), of which she is currently the vice president (I am also a member of the Executive Council of the FDIF).
>
> She is a beautiful young woman in my opinion, always impeccably dressed in very sober, but pretty, dresses. She is a symbol of modern woman: in a body which seems so fragile, so much courage and energy.

Rahantavololona Andriamanjato is a woman also widely admired, by both men and women, for her beauty, charm, and inner strength, no less than for her remarkable professional achievements. With all the controversy raging these days about where women should spend their time—in the kitchen or in the office—she seems to have found some good answers:

> My children (three boys, one girl) do not see me very much. But they are used to having parents who are almost always in conferences or travelling. But in the final analysis, it is not the quantity of time that we pass with them that is important, but the quality.
>
> We try, the days that we are with them, to make them understand also that what we are doing is not for ourselves but for them, so that they will live in a better world, a world of

peace and of brotherhood, that their view of the world not be limited to the four walls of our house, but that they participate also, if only in thought, in the different struggles against injustice and for the liberty of Vietnam, South Africa, the Portuguese colonies, Palestine, South America, Southeast Asia, etc. And naturally, even though they are only six to eleven years old, they are also concerned with the problems of our country and are learning that the goal of life is not "to become rich" but "to be useful to society." This is the heritage that my husband and I leave to them.*

The once peaceful island of Madagascar is in turmoil at this writing, its conservative President Tsiranana repudiated in a student-triggered revolt against French-oriented curriculum and neglect of Malagasy tradition and culture. With the government temporarily in the hands of the army, no one can predict the final outcome or the role of the Andriamanjatos in Madagascar's future. But we can be sure that Rahantavololona Andriamanjato and her husband, wherever and however they can, will continue working unstintingly for the better life they want for their children and all the other future citizens of the world. Perhaps it is time for Mrs. Andriamanjato to assume another of her names, Razanamahandry, "she who is patient."

The Water-Seeker
FLAVIEN RANAIVO

A Dove is she
who goes down
the rocky path
sliding like

* Translated from a letter written in French by Mrs. Andriamanjato.

a capricious pebble
on the steep slope
towards the spring.

The water-seeker.

She descends
with clumsy care,
catching
time and again
with one hand
on the aloe leaves
smooth and pointed,
with the other
she holds the earthen pitcher
—of the country earth—
Scarcely sure
those naked
feet
of the girl of Imerina.
What can she be dreaming
beneath her thick lamba
which yet moulds,
breasts half guessed, sharp
smooth and pointed?
—"What can you be dreaming
Amber-skinned one
Almond-eyed one?"—
What can she be thinking
she-who-has-never-known
nor joy nor sorrow
nor love nor hate . . .

Alluring yet
those lying lips:
so smooth and pointed?
A breath,
the breath of a breeze
has so soon ruffled
her black hair.
What can she be dreaming
this soul-less body
which ruffles
the soul of the poet?
Sweet
deceit.*

* Flavien Ranaivo, "The Water-Seeker," translated from the French by Dorothy Blair, *African Voices* (Madagascar), ed. Peggy Rutherfoord, Grosset's Universal Library, p. 102.

SOUTH AFRICA

Joyce Sikhakane
Winnie Mandela

An Agony
—BY JOYCE SIKHAKANE

My head is heavy, my shoulders shrug,
because despite
all my eyes have seen
my head has said
my heart has felt,
I do not believe
that White, Black and Yellow
cannot talk, walk, eat, kiss and share.

It worries me to think
that only people of my colour

will liberate me.

You mustn't trust a white man
my grandfather used to tell me
when I was a child.
You mustn't think a White man cares for you
my people caution me.
You know when a White man wants to know you?
When you bring him money!

The Indians? He's black as you.
But, not as poor as you.
He knows his trade—cheating you.
He's happy to lend you money
just forgets to mention
the twenty per cent interest!
until you have to pay it.

And the Coloured? I ask.
Ag! Him, they say.
He doesn't know where he stands,
But he prefers his skin whitest
And his hair straightest.
And somehow forgets the second names
of his black and kinky cousins!

I know of Whites, Coloureds and Indians
who are not like that, I say.
But, I'm told they are only a few.

Now, what about you, my fellow African.
We are intimidated, they say
Modimo, we're very very busy, they say,
not losing

our passes,
our birth certificates,
our train tickets,
our rent receipts
our urban residential permits,
(not to mention our money, our husbands and our lives).

My head is heavy, my shoulders shrug,
because despite
all my eyes have seen
my head has said
my heart has felt,
I do not believe
that White, Black and Yellow
cannot talk, walk, eat, kiss and share.*

So weeps a black woman over her homeland, physically one of the
most beautiful countries in Africa, but in terms of human relations
one of the ugliest in the world. As Joyce Sikhakane tells it here, the
system of "apartheid," meaning "separate development" and pro-
nounced, significantly, "apart-*hate*," sets all of the various racial
groups which have settled in South Africa against each other. This
system, created and enforced by the country's whites—who, though
numbering less than a fifth of the total population, claim all the best
land and completely control the government—classifies all people according to skin color: whites, persons of European origin, dominated
by the Afrikaners (descendants of Early Dutch settlers); Africans or
"Bantu," persons of African descent; "colored," those of racially
mixed descent; and Asians, persons of Asian (mostly Indian) descent.
Color label determines where a person lives, what kind of job he can

---

* *Anti-Apartheid News.*

hold, where he goes to school, whether or not he can own property, whom he can marry, and even where he can be buried. Color classification can get very technical, depending on how vital you are to the South African economy: e.g., Chinese people are classed as "colored," while the equally yellow-skinned people from Japan, which has important trade relations with South Africa, pass as honorary "whites." Also white people with deep suntans sometimes get into trouble, for only a person legally classed as "white" can enjoy the full privileges of the land.

As Joyce Sikhakane tells it above, Africans fare the worst; plagued daily with constant demands for passes, receipts, and other officially required documents, their life is totally regulated by a government in which they have no voice.

Because she dares to question these ridiculous laws of South Africa, Joyce Sikhakane has spent much of her time the past few years in jail or under house arrest. She is one of many African women involved in the struggle for liberation from this regime; some, like her and Winnie Mandela, work inside the country; others, like Brigalia Bam and Miriam Makeba—whose stories follow—try to rally support from the outside. The "agony" of the poem is well known to all, but so are the inspiring words of the great leader Nelson Mandela, spoken just before he was sentenced to life imprisonment on Robben Island:

> During my lifetime I have dedicated myself to this struggle of the African people. I have fought against White domination, and I have fought against Black domination. I have cherished the ideal of a democratic and free society in which all persons live together in harmony and with equal opportunities. It is an ideal which I hope to live for and to achieve. But if needs be it is an ideal for which I am prepared to die.*

* Nelson Mandela, *No Easy Walk to Freedom*, Heinemann Educational Books, p. 189.

Before his imprisonment in 1964, Nelson Mandela had served as head of the African National Congress (ANC), the African liberation movement originally founded by the famous Nobel Peace Prize winner, Chief Albert Luthuli. Although the ANC is banned in South Africa today, its branches in exile continue the struggle.

Mandela's beautiful wife, Winnie, left alone with their three children and rarely allowed to visit her husband in jail, has nevertheless carried on his work in the country. Her courage and determination in the face of constant harassment by government officials, frequent detention on glibly invented charges, and house arrest, has given heart to many others. For a period of fifteen months—from May, 1969, to October, 1970—Winnie Mandela, Joyce Sikhakane, and nineteen others (including three other women) were held in confinement without access to lawyers or to their families; they were charged with various "subversive" activities, all neatly fitted under the Suppression of Communism Act. In an article written after their release the ANC magazine *Sechaba* (November–December, 1970) described what it termed "A Trial of Inner Strength":

The marathon trial of Winnie Mandela and her 19 co-accused ended in a wave of excitement and exultation throughout South Africa. Wherever the oppressed heard the news there was the deepest feeling of relief that this brave group, with the exception of Benjamin Ramotse who remained in custody, was finally released.

The universal exultation ought not to allow us to forget the great courage and fortitude of Winnie Mandela who triumphed against the terrorism of the Special Branch. Neither torture nor blandishments could break their spirit nor induce them to turn against their co-accused. Facing the most serious charges under the Terrorism Act, they held out against the relentless vindictiveness of the prosecution in its determination to get a conviction. The torturers failed. They more than met their match in the inner strength of Winnie Mandela's group.

Mrs. Mandela was acquitted, but just as she was leaving to visit her husband at Robben Island—her first visit with him in over eighteen months—she was put under house arrest again.

The full stories of Winnie Mandela, of Joyce Sikhakane, of Dorothy Nyembe (an African woman now serving a fifty-year prison sentence on the same kind of "subversive" charges), and of many other brave women risking their lives daily to liberate their people, should be told here. They are great women, beautiful and compassionate. But, because of the ever-lurking vigilantes of South Africa, who can turn the most innocent act or statement into a pretext for arrest, the privacy of these women must be respected. We can only salute them now.

Brigalia Bam

Brigalia Bam, schoolmate of Winnie Mandela, is one of those talented and brave black women of South Africa who have found ways of serving the cause of freedom outside their homeland. Her job as head of a special working group at the World Council of Churches (based in Geneva), dealing with women and youth, carries her all over the world, and she is often called upon to discuss the problems of her country. In 1969 the World Council of Churches made a direct commitment to the liberation struggle by allocating funds to organizations fighting racism in South Africa.

Ordinarily animated and bubbling with humor, Brigalia stiffens and a shadow crosses her face when anyone asks her when she plans to see her family. Her mother works in Natal; a brother, like Nelson Mandela, is a political prisoner at Robben Island near Cape Town.

Brigalia Bam was born on April 21, 1933, in the Transkei, a section in the southeast part of the country, bounded on one side by the Indian Ocean. It is one of the most picturesque areas of South Africa, a land of rolling hills and streams, rich grazing and farm country, small round huts—rondavels—dotting the hills. Although the government selected the Transkei in 1955 as the first of its Bantustan experiments—reserving it as a semi-independent black territory for the approximately 2½ million members of the Xosa group—it excluded many of the best farming lands from the reserve; these were long ago taken over by whites. Umtata, capital of Transkei, Port St. John, the only developed seaport, and all seashore resorts of any quality are also reserved for whites only.

As African children go, Brigalia Bam was among the privileged, coming from several generations of educated people. Both parents were teachers, as was her grandfather, an important influence on her life. Brigalia's father, Lockington Bam, worked as both teacher and civil servant up to the time of his death in 1952. Her mother, Temperance Bam, was a teacher before her marriage, and after her children were older took courses in health education. After her husband's death Mrs. Bam began work in the Polela Health Center in Natal, a province north of the Transkei. This center was started by the government as a pilot training center in preventive medicine in the late 1940's and has been mentioned in a number of medical books. Mrs. Bam continues to work there today.

From the age of seven Brigalia attended a private boarding school, run by Anglican nuns from Scotland, where she stayed until she was thirteen. It is the nuns of this school that she credits with giving her a firm spiritual basis for her life.

"They were not overly pious," Brigalia remembers, "because they taught us folk dancing, tennis and basketball. But more important, they provided models which, consciously or unconsciously, we tried to emulate. I believe this is very necessary for young people."

Another important influence was her grandfather, a Methodist layman who earned his living as a teacher and civil servant. Because he

Miss Brigalia Bam.

was a very outgoing person, deeply concerned for the welfare of people, he was also—at least by avocation—a social worker. He had some advanced ideas about women: in a time and place where African women were considered chiefly in terms of *lobola* (bride price) and child-raising, he believed firmly that women needed to obtain an education of a broader sort. In fact he required each of his daughters to take professional training before she could marry.

"For someone of his generation he was very unusual," says Brigalia.

So, in the family tradition, she, too, decided to do social work. During high school days Brigalia often accompanied her mother on home visits in which she taught African women the principles of homemaking—nutrition, child care, cooking, and sewing. It was through these visits that Brigalia Bam was struck with the desperate need of women for education and a better standard of living. This experience also convinced her that those who had received an education had a moral obligation to use their training for the benefit of the total community.

Free public education was then, and still is, available to white children in South Africa but not to blacks. Even though her parents earned less than white teachers, they had to pay for her education; nevertheless, like many other African parents, Mr. and Mrs. Bam were glad to make the sacrifice, feeling education would prove an avenue of liberation for their daughter.

Shawbury Institution, the high school which Brigalia attended, was church sponsored, as was the school to which she went after graduation: Lovedale Teacher Training College. Following that, a "Martha Washington Scholarship" provided by Congregational churches in the U.S.A. enabled her to attend the Jan Hofmeyr School of Social Work in Johannesburg, where she earned a diploma.

Winnie Mandela—not yet married to the ANC leader—was among her schoolmates at the Jan Hofmeyr School (named for a well-known Afrikaner statesman). She was a class ahead of Brigalia and already an established leader with a reputation for uncanny ability to size up people and their potentialities for development. According to another Jan Hofmeyr alumna, who knows both Winnie and Brigalia, Winnie Mandela singled out the newcomer from the Transkei as a person of unusual gifts, destined for an important leadership role. This turned out to be entirely true, even though most of Brigalia Bam's recognition came from outside her country.

Following graduation at Jan Hofmeyr, Brigalia served for two years as youth secretary for the YWCA of Natal and Zululand, based in Durban. Here she had responsibility for work among "Y Teens" and young adults. As a result of her interest in the Durban Committee on Child Welfare, she was elected chairman of the African Child Welfare Society. Following her first job came four years of work with women as well as youth in the province of Natal and Zululand. Finally the YWCA made an opening possible at the national level and for three years Brigalia was national executive secretary of the world-affiliated YWCA of South Africa. Together with the Council of Churches, the YWCA and other youth groups offered training for leaders of youth groups on an ecumenical—i.e., worldwide—basis. Through the Council of Churches and the All Africa Conference of Churches, Brigalia Bam made contact with the World Council of Churches, based in Geneva.

Through these years of working in her own country Brigalia experienced all the frustrations of the apartheid system. While she was growing up, because of her parents' sacrifices for her education, she had always felt under tremendous pressure to prove her worth as a person. She herself was led to believe, as did her parents, that if she achieved the status of a professional, she would be free to participate in the affairs of the nation. But this did not happen.

Her disappointment and frustration got greater. The more opportunity a black person had for education, the more he felt discriminated against in jobs, housing, public services.

"We drove ourselves to achieve and then didn't get rewarded," is
the way Brigalia put it.

When she moved to Durban to work at the YWCA Brigalia's first
problem was to find suitable housing. White colleagues had no problem in this respect. Nor could she get the same salary as whites, even
though she had the same qualifications and held a responsible job.

The hardest thing to bear was the fact that she was refused the use
of facilities such as toilets.

"Just because we were black we could not go to the toilet in a restaurant. After driving for miles we were permitted to buy gas but
could not get tea in the adjoining restaurant or use the toilet," she reports. "This denial of basic human needs was the worst."

Today the situation is even worse, she believes, because more Africans are somehow improving their living standard a little and they
threaten the whites. Apartheid has hardened as a result of white fears.

Brigalia Bam's first contact with the World Council of Churches
opened many new avenues. Through this organization she participated in several work camps—two outside of South Africa and one
within her own country. Also through the World Council she had a
chance to train leaders of church youth groups in Tanzania. In 1962
she attended the All Africa Youth Assembly in Nairobi, which led to
her being named the next year as a youth delegate to the All Africa
Conference of Churches (AACC) meeting at Kampala, Uganda.
Earlier she had served on the AACC's Youth Commission and on the
Youth Committee of the Natal Christian Council. At the All African
Conference of Churches meeting in Kampala in 1963 she was appointed to the AACC Executive Committee, one of three women so
named.

"This shocked everyone," Brigalia recalls, "both because we were women and I was a youth delegate."

Shock turned quickly into respect as the young South African proceeded in her refreshingly honest and forthright way to bring new insights to AACC deliberations, particularly in regard to the role of women. Male chauvinists, whether African-oriented or European-oriented, were not lacking in these ecumenical circles; but many of them were disarmed. Her charm, sense of humor, and obvious feminine assets made them take notice, but they were not prepared for her uncompromising assault on outworn ideas and traditions.

In September, 1967, Brigalia joined the World Council of Churches staff in Geneva, Switzerland, in what was then known as the Department of Cooperation of Men and Women in Church, Family, and Society. There were some jokes about the rather ponderous title of this department and Brigalia herself went along good-naturedly with some teasing about her role in the "affairs" of men and women. But it was soon apparent that she was out to make changes. In her first announcement she said she would not strive to build stronger women's organizations in the World Council of Churches (WCC) member churches, but would seek instead ways in which women could make a contribution to the total church. She stressed the need for changed attitudes in the church with respect to women, urging the WCC to take the lead.

A consultation she arranged on the ordination of women established that there was little justification in the Bible for refusing to ordain women as priests and pastors.

Today the department has been reorganized and Brigalia Bam heads the Staff Working Group on Renewal and Renewal Movements, the major components being women and youth. In this capacity she continues to deal with the issue of discrimination against women, prodding women to take the initiative themselves.

"Traditionally we said that women were the ones responsible for the family," says Brigalia, "but this was viewing women's role in too narrow a focus."

She therefore concentrates on women's leadership training seminars on the several continents where women are made aware of what is happening in the world and are enabled to participate more fully in church, civic, and political affairs. The picture taken at such a seminar held in April, 1972, for women of East, Central, and Southern Africa

Miss Brigalia Bam and Princess Elizabeth of Toro.

L.M.B. WAMALA, KAMPAL

(at Kampala, Uganda), demonstrates the variety of women participating: shown conversing with Miss Bam is Princess Elizabeth of Toro, Uganda's "Roving Ambassador" and a former model and movie actress. Many of the seminars include information on family planning and the changing roles of men and women in the marriage relationship. Miss Bam has also planned with Roman Catholic women's groups seminars on the role of women in the mass media and in education for world peace.

Brigalia Bam believes firmly that women have vast reservoirs of power that have not been tapped in most parts of the world, and that the Christian church can be an important instrument in encouraging the use of such power. In a recent article, written for a special issue of *New World Outlook*, she said:

> We need a church that will proclaim women's rights unafraid and courageous despite culture's slowness in emerging from the twilight of male privilege and dominance.*

An unusually articulate and forceful speaker, Miss Bam has been in great demand at national conferences and assemblies. She has addressed the World Federation of Methodist Women at Denver, Colorado (1971), the Church Workers' Assembly in Derby, England (1971), the National Meeting of United Presbyterian Women at Purdue, Indiana (1970), the Women's Assembly at Mikelli, Finland (1969), and the European Consultation on Laymen Abroad (1969). In numerous women's seminars she has spoken on such World Council concerns as racism, development, and barriers to ecumenism. She has written articles for *New World Outlook*, *Oekumenische Rundschau*,

* *New World Outlook*, April, 1971, p. 10.

World Christian Education, and the Advent booklet of the World Alliance of Reformed Churches.

Though forced by the cruel laws of her homeland to live and work outside South Africa, it is never far from her mind or concern. Wherever she is, she rarely fails to make a passionate plea against racism, the cancer that has so wrecked her country and threatens every country in the world. Unlike some, however, Brigalia does not believe the situation of blacks in the U.S.A. and in South Africa is comparable. Despite racial tension and injustice in the U.S.A., she points out, the laws here are on the side of blacks. Efforts are being made, even in the church, to give them responsible positions. Also U.S. blacks can protest and demonstrate against injustices. Through the mass media they can tell the world, and this provides some psychological outlet. The South African situation is the opposite. All laws deny opportunities to Africans: the Group Area Act, job reservation, land ownership, the police—all are against blacks. Television is denied to everyone in South Africa, for fear of contaminating influences from outside; there is some talk now of government-controlled programs in the future. Blacks have no voice anywhere save in the liberation movements, forced to operate in secret; at present all Africans in South Africa are virtual slaves.

Brigalia Bam points out that the majority of those belonging to liberation movements and working outside South Africa are Christians. They have been driven to fight for justice because all other methods have been tried and failed. Ironically, some of the church leaders in South Africa have been the blindest to the meaning of Christian love and have even twisted Scripture to support racist policies. Dissenting white ministers, such as Trevor Huddleston and ffrench-Beytagh, and white liberals such as Alan Paton (also a minister), and the courageous woman member of parliament, Helen Suzman, have been unable to "break the yoke of enslavement." Thus blacks now see that only they can bring liberation.

However, they still count on the support of all, black and white, who are willing to join the fight. There are a number of ways—positive and negative—Miss Bam suggests, in which the U.S. can help:

> Beginning with the Americans withdrawing investments in South Africa, my hope would be that then there would be some kind of discussion arising out of the withdrawal, since both the U.S. and South Africa have the race problem in common.

As it is, American investments, amounting to well over $900 million in 1968, actually support the ideology of apartheid. Clearly, says Brigalia—and most people agree with her on this point—the economic system cannot continue to operate without outside support. Through cheap African labor South Africa carries out the worst form of exploitation and American firms profit from it. Some people argue that U.S. investment helps to develop the country and therefore benefits the Africans; others point out that African people here enjoy a higher living standard than elsewhere on the continent. No, says Brigalia—and many people who really know the situation agree with her—it is only the owners and managers, all white, who really profit from the investments. Prosperity stops at the boundaries of the cities; as soon as you get into the townships and reserves you see that few of the benefits trickle down to the masses of people. While it is true that some blacks do enjoy a higher living standard than elsewhere in Africa, most of them would gladly give up any material benefits they have in exchange for real freedom to determine their own destiny. For blacks and whites alike, the old Scripture saying still holds:

For what is a man profited, if he shall gain the whole world,
and lose his own soul? (Matthew 16:26)

Wherever Africans are gathered today, at student rallies, meetings
of the African National Congress, or in small groups in homes, two
songs are sung that have special meaning. One, *"Nkosi Sikelele"*
("God Bless Africa") has long been known as a sort of African national anthem, which originated in South Africa; many individual
countries, such as Tanzania and Zambia, have used its music—composed by a Zulu pastor/schoolteacher—for their own national an-
thems. Another, *"Mayibuye i Afrika,"* is a song that has special significance for black South Africans: "Africa must come back to us."

This is the hope of Brigalia Bam, of Miriam Makeba, Winnie
Mandela, Joyce Sikhakane, Dorothy Nyembe, and the countless other
brave women of South Africa: that some day—within their lifetime,
perhaps—they and all the other Africans may enjoy the full privileges
of their ancestral land. Until they do there is no real peace or joy for
any of us, black or white. Mazisi Kunene, a Zulu poet and leader of
the African National Congress, sums it up this way:

> Why should those at the end of the earth
> Not drink from the same calabash
> And build their homes in the valley of the earth
> And together grow with our children? *

* Mazisi Kunene, *Zulu Poems*, "Mother Earth or the Folly of National Boundaries," New
York, Africana Publishing Corporation, 1970, p. 45.

Miriam Makeba

When she first ambled on stage, the young African girl with the closely cropped hair seemed strangely out of place amid the sophistication of New York's Blue Angel supper club. But when doe-eyed Miriam Makeba began running through her exotic bag of Zulu, Xosa, and other folk songs, it was with the polish and finesse of a seasoned night-club performer. She sang with the smoky tones and delicate phrasing of Ella Fitzgerald and when the occasion demanded, she summoned up the brassy showmanship of Ethel Merman and the intimate warmth of Frank Sinatra. When she moved it was with the insistent rhythm of a tribal dance.

Forty minutes after she launched her performance, the 27-year-old Xosa tribeswoman quietly slid off stage. The hush that had fallen over the glittering audience was broken by a torrent of applause and cheers. Harry Belafonte, who had to stand against an upholstered wall in the rear, shouted, "Great,

great!" Lauren Bacall leaned across her ashtray-sized table and clapped her hands together thunderously. After Miriam had taken her sixth and final bow, Belafonte, who was one of her discoverers, said flatly, "She is easily the most revolutionary new talent to appear in any medium in the last decade." *

This was a *Newsweek* reporter's version of a story making headlines in all the papers in the first months of 1960. New Yorkers were dumbfounded by the new singing star from Africa. They didn't know what to make of Miriam Makeba, so they compared her to all their own singing greats. But, as a *Time* reporter had to admit, "she sings like no one else." In the same article he described her as "the most exciting new talent to appear in many years." ** *The New York Times Magazine* (February 28, 1960) ran a feature article about her.

"The trouble is," wrote *Time* magazine, "that she wants to go home—home being a four-room house in Mofolo village, a South African 'location' (Negro reservation) outside Johannesburg." ***

The home that Miriam Makeba had left, only a few months before this sensational U.S. debut, offered nothing of the glamor and acclaim bestowed on her unquestioningly here and at the Venice Film Festival the preceding summer.

"Down there," said Miriam, speaking sadly but fondly of South Africa, "if you aren't white, you may be a star, but you're still nothing. But I still want to go home."

Today, almost fifteen years later, Miriam Makeba still cannot go home. Even to sing there she would have to perform for separate audiences of black and white, and that, of course, she would never do again. And because she has become one of Africa's most outspoken

* *Newsweek*, Feb. 1, 1960, p. 84.

** *Time*, Feb. 1, 1960, p. 52.

*** *Ibid.*

critics of "apartheid," the South African government's "separate de-velopment" policy which discriminates extremely unfairly against blacks, Miriam Makeba, like thousands of her countrymen, must live in virtual exile. There are many laws and zealous enforcers of laws conveniently available to trap such dissenters the moment they try to return to South Africa.

Only a few months after her successful debut in the United States, on March 21, 1960, Miriam Makeba's aunt and three cousins were massacred along with 65 others during a demonstration at Sharpeville near Johannesburg; some 20,000 Africans were protesting a law that requires every black person in South Africa to carry a passbook, a cumbersome document revealing every detail of his personal life, which everyone over 16 must show in order to travel, to establish res-idence, get a job, or even to exist legally. Although the protesters made it clear their move was nonviolent, stating, "We are willing to die for our freedom; we are not yet ready to kill for it," the govern-ment's answer was very plain. With no warning at all, the police opened fire on the crowd, killing 69 of them immediately and wound-ing some 257 others; all were detained without trial. And today the *"dom pas"* (Afrikaner word for "stupid passbook") is still a fact of daily life for all black South Africans.

The love match that began in 1960 between Miriam Makeba and the U.S.A. has somewhat cooled in the past few years, especially since she married the controversial American civil rights leader, Stokely Carmichael. In 1960 she told *The New York Times*, "Any American who has been to South Africa would know very well what I'd say about New York. There's no comparison. . . ." But in early 1972, during a TV interview with the black poet, Nikki Giovanni, she said she felt South Africa and America's attitudes toward the blacks were the same. "In South Africa," she said, "they are more honest; there they admit to being what they are."

Miriam Makeba speaking with Acting Secretary-General U Thant on the occasion of United Nations Staff Day.

However others may agree or disagree with her in comparing racial situations here and elsewhere, Miriam Makeba remains today a person entirely true to her convictions, as well as a supreme artist.

"I am interested in saying the truth," she declared quietly to Miss Giovanni, "even if it hurts."

Only those who have lived under the system of apartheid—and particularly the black people, who have experienced the worst of its enslavement—can fully understand why Miriam Makeba and others feel there is no room for compromise in the fight against it.

For, in spite of years of world condemnation of its inhumanity, the South African government continues to deny basic rights and privileges to its nonwhite citizens. Blacks, or Africans, who outnumber whites over four to one, cannot vote, cannot own land, and have very restricting laws about where they can live, eat, work, or travel.

As an African, child of Xosa parents (related to the Zulus), Miriam Makeba came into the system at the lowest rung of the ladder, a heavy chain of rules and regulations restricting every minute of her life and that of all her family. Her father, a schoolteacher, had two choices of where to live: either a rural tribal reservation on poor, uncultivable soil, or a government regulated township near a city. He chose the latter, and after obtaining government permission, moved into Prospect township near Johannesburg. This was a segregated "shantytown" for "Bantu" people only, situated some distance from the all-white city; black people could go into Johannesburg to work but only on buses designated especially for them and they had to leave the city by a certain time each evening. The house where Zenzi Miriam Makeba was born, on March 4, 1932, was, like all the others in Prospect reservation, small and cheaply built, with no electricity or running water, crowded in a dismal row along unshaded, narrow streets. There was little space here for children to play.

The meager salary Miriam's father drew for his teaching was not enough to pay the rent and keep the family supplied in mealie meal; as an African, he could not own land. So Miriam's mother went into the city to work as a maid in a white house, forced to tend well-fed, starched, and carefully sheltered white children, while her own children—Miriam and a younger brother and sister, Joseph and Mizpah —had to get along without her.

For Miriam and her African playmates there were no free public schools as there were for white children. When she was of school age she attended Kilnerton Training Institute, a Methodist school for Africans, located in Pretoria. Pretoria, only a short distance from Johannesburg, is the administrative capital of South Africa; Cape Town, at the southwestern tip of the continent, is its legislative capital. According to the noted South African author, Alan Paton:

> If the handiwork of man is to be considered, as it should be in the making of a city, then Pretoria is the most beautiful of South African cities. The people of Pretoria are true gardeners, and even now in this winter month of June can be seen traces of their wonderful rose gardens. These trees that we see lining so many streets are the jacarandas; they flower in October and November, and in cool dull weather the blue blossoms drop and lie unfaded on the ground, giving to the streets a fantastic beauty.*

But, because she was black, Miriam Makeba was shut off from much of this beauty; nevertheless, at Kilnerton Institute she found beauty of another kind. Music had always been a consuming passion; as a small child she listened and joined in the traditional songs of her people, punctuated with the many varieties of clicks characteristic of Xosa and Zulu languages; other music she learned from hours of listening to the radio or to phonograph records. Some of her favorite recordings were those of American jazz musicians, especially Ella Fitzgerald.

---

* Alan Paton, *Land and People of South Africa*, Philadelphia, J. B. Lippincott Company, Rev. 1972, p. 82.

"Anyone who sings," she later told an interviewer, "makes music, as long as it's good to my ear." Miriam's own singing gifts were soon recognized at Kilnerton and through the school choirs she had her first chance to perform in public. At the age of thirteen she sang her first solo before a microphone, for King George VI of England when he visited South Africa.

After eight years at the Methodist school, Miriam Makeba joined her mother as a servant in private white homes of Johannesburg. An early marriage resulted in the birth of a small daughter, Bongi (Angela), but her husband died when Miriam was still only nineteen. With a baby to support, she had to keep working as a maid; however in her spare time Miriam began to do a lot of singing at weddings, funerals, and benefits. In 1954, when she was twenty-two, she had her first professional engagement; a group of eleven male singers, known as the Black Manhattan Brothers, invited her to become their female vocalist. For the next three years she toured with this group, traveling by bus and making one-night stands throughout South Africa, Rhodesia, and the Belgian Congo (now known as Zaire). Often the bus broke down, meaning long hot waits far from food and shelter. Miriam recalls that at first she was "crying all the time," but it did not take her long to learn that "the show must go on." Following this, she toured with a musical variety show and began making many personal appearances. These and her popular recordings soon made the name of Miriam Makeba well known in South Africa; even though she received no royalties herself, her records were best sellers. It was her performance of the leading role in a jazz opera, *King Kong*, in early 1959, which firmly established her reputation and brought her to international attention.

In *King Kong*, based on a true story of a prizefighter who killed his mistress, Miss Makeba played the role of Joyce, owner of a "shebeen," an African drinking place, illegal in South Africa. Because of apartheid regulations, the production had to play to separate black and white audiences. Performances for black audiences were often given under extremely difficult circumstances: e.g., special arrangements had to be made for transportation of the audience, and they were restricted to small halls with bad acoustics. In beautiful, all-white Pretoria the production was banned altogether. In spite of this, *King Kong* toured the country with extraordinary success for eight months; in Cape Town whites lined up at dawn to buy seats—there were no vacancies. Black and white audiences everywhere cheered the electrifying performance of the young star, Miriam Makeba. "Back of the Moon" and other songs she introduced in the show became best-selling records.

Before her successful appearance in *King Kong*, Miriam Makeba had played the female lead and sung two songs in a movie called *Come Back, Africa*, made in 1958. For obvious reasons this film had not been shown in South Africa. Lionel Rogosin, an independent American film maker, had produced and directed the movie on location in Sofiatown, a Bantu reservation outside Johannesburg which was being torn down to make way for an all-white suburb. Although, at the time he was making the film, Rogosin gave the impression to South African authorities that he was doing a simple sort of travelogue to show the "quaint" folkways of the African people, his real motive was quite different. *Come Back, Africa* turned out to be an antiapartheid semi-documentary, intended to show the world the unjust treatment of black people by the South African government. The movie was smuggled out of the country and shown at the Venice Film Festival in 1959, where it drew very favorable notices; film audiences were particularly enthusiastic about the performance of Miriam Makeba. So, in the summer of 1959, she was invited to make a personal appearance at the festival.

Two years before, feeling restless and with vague notions of traveling abroad, Miriam Makeba had applied for a passport. Though the government had been slow in granting it, giving her flimsy excuses each time she inquired, she had finally obtained it by the time of the Venice invitation. With no idea of the international acclaim awaiting her in Europe, she intended the trip to be just a brief holiday. In spite of the oppressive laws of South Africa, there was still much to hold her in her homeland: a widowed mother, her eight-year-old daughter Bongi, a second husband (Sonny Pillay, a ballad singer of Indian ex-

From left to right: *Alan King (comedian), Theodore Bikel (folk singer), Miriam Makeba (singer), U Thant (Acting Secretary-General), Byron Janis (pianist), Tony Randall (master of ceremonies), Duke Ellington (bandleader), and Aldo Parisot (cellist) on the occasion of United Nations Staff Day.*

traction, from whom she was later divorced), and many other relatives dear to her. But from the minute she landed in Venice, Miriam Makeba's life was not her own. As she said later, "I never know what I'm going to do . . . all these things happen to me. I never plan ahead."

Venice devoured her. Several American entertainers at the festival —among them Steve Allen—were captivated by her and planned to bring her to the United States. In London she met Harry Belafonte, who became her chief sponsor and mentor; on November 30, 1959, she made her American debut on the nationally televised Steve Allen Show.

The shy African girl arrived at Idlewild (now Kennedy) Airport in New York on November 11, a few days before her debut, somewhat dazed by all that had happened to her. Like all newcomers to the huge American city, Miriam Makeba was taken sightseeing: to the Empire State Building, the Statue of Liberty, Radio City, all the fashionable stores on Fifth Avenue. Harlem fascinated her, but she would not go there: "Maybe that would remind me of home," she said wistfully. "One thing I know . . . when I got here I expected them (the blacks) to speak to me in Zulu."

She had some fears about the American public, whose jazz greats had been her models so many years. Speaking of her qualms later to a reporter, she confessed: "I didn't know whether people would like my singing. This was terrible."

Everyone knows now, of course, that she had no reason to be afraid, for from the first moment when she stepped to the stage of the Steve Allen Show, she was a sensation. Soon afterward she was booked into the Village Vanguard, a well-known nightclub in Greenwich Village, New York City, and from there to one of New York's most fashionable East Side nightclubs, the sophisticated Blue Angel— which had launched such stars as Pearl Bailey and Eartha Kitt. By

February, 1960, barely three months after her arrival in the United States, Miriam Makeba was earning $750 a week, more than a year's earnings for the majority of her people back home.

At the time of her United States debut, the African look was not as popular as it is today: American blacks still called themselves "Negro," spent thousands of dollars on straightening their hair, and dressed conventionally "white" style. Nightclub entertainers went in for a bit more glitter, but the exotic African styles introduced in the later sixties—after Afro-Americans began showing pride in their heritage—were then unknown. Though she, too, wore conventional European clothes most of the time, Miriam Makeba's short-cropped woolly hair and long dangling earrings drew stares. With her huge expressive eyes and slender grace, everyone recognized her as an extraordinarily beautiful woman, but at that time it was felt necessary to make her "presentable" for American audiences. Two of her new friends, Harry Belafonte and Diahann Carroll, themselves the most glamorous of stars, took her in hand. Wisely, they did not try to change Miriam's natural hairdo, but they hired a dress designer, and otherwise gave Western polish to the rough African diamond. Among other things they taught her to wait until the audience had quieted down before beginning a song; in Africa, one doesn't expect such undivided attention. At her debut some of the critics noted the contrast between her sleek Fifth Avenue gown and her simple African manner. As she became better established, and as African style became more generally accepted, Miriam Makeba asserted her own individual taste. Today she usually wears straight-lined, floor-length sheaths, sometimes flowing African-style garments, in exotic colors. Except for long dangling earrings, she seldom wears jewelry. While she can stir an audience to a frenzy of excitement, her stage presence is generally elegant and simple.

But it was neither her beauty nor her stage presence that provoked the wild applause at her debut, interviews by all the major journals and newspapers, and nationwide demand for her appearances. The astonishing range of her voice—from high, pure, and flutelike tones to powerful trumpet calls or gutty earth sounds—and her amazing versatility of expression enthralled everyone. The African singer could make you laugh, cry, shout, or send chills down your spine, all within the space of a few minutes.

She had had no formal training, could not read music, and yet her repertoire included music from all over the world and she performed it in an amazing variety of styles and languages. There were songs from her homeland that her mother had taught her, Yiddish songs learned from a Jewish producer in South Africa, folk music, calypso, and jazz absorbed from hours of listening to radio and records. She could deliver a ballad in clean, classic style, mystify an audience with one of her "click" songs—where she brought forth a torrent of rhythmic clicks from somewhere deep inside her mouth and throat without ever seeming to move a muscle—or bring people to their feet with the way she sang a jazz selection. Carefully schooled musicians were astounded at her ability to do things instinctively which most people take years to learn, if at all. For example, on a record later produced by Belafonte, Miriam Makeba sang with herself in "many voices" two songs to demonstrate how a group of Africans would sing them. After making one recording, she dubbed in seven other recordings—by means of two multitracks—one at a time, each time listening to herself on the original recording. The result in each case was something that sounded like an African chorus, weaving in many cross rhythms and embellishments. According to Belafonte, when Miss Makeba did this recording there were no retakes, no mistakes.

Since her music was unwritten, the American musicians had to learn the African songs through hours of listening to her sing the lyrics and beat out the rhythms. One of the first instrumental trios to ap-

pear with her regularly was composed of Sam Brown, guitar, Bill
Salter, bass, and Auchee Lee, drums and flute. Belafonte himself made
many of her musical arrangements, and booked her for national and
international tours. She was the first featured performer he had ever
allowed to share top billing with him.

Since 1960 Miss Makeba has made many record albums, for RCA
Victor and other major companies all over the world, and has toured
from continent to continent. During these thirteen years her repertoire has grown constantly, including English ballads, jazz, nightclub
songs, South American bossa novas, West Indian calypso, Hebrew
and Yiddish melodies, Haitian chants, and other folk songs from all
over the world. At a nightclub one evening someone asked her why
she did not sing any of the Afrikaner *lietjes,* folk tunes of the white
Dutch settlers of South Africa. Although she knew the Afrikaans language well, she replied: "When they sing in my language, I will sing
in theirs."

At first, fearing for the safety of her daughter and other relatives
back home, she refused to talk about the political situation in South
Africa. But many of her songs, particularly one called "Wimoweh,"
reflected her deep feeling for her people. "Wimoweh" is a Zulu lion-
hunting song and Miss Makeba's interpretation of it left no doubt that
the "lion" was the South African government.

"One day," she told a columnist of a Washington paper (*Washington Post and Times-Herald*, June 25, 1961), "we are going to kill that
lion." Jerry Tallmer, reviewing a performance in September, 1963,
for the *New York Post*, described her singing of "Wimoweh" thus:

> First a lull, and then a croon, and then a gathering glory,
> and then the arm going up with the spear and the body afire
> and the lion coming in and the joy going out, through the
> spear, the arm, the deep-set glowing eyes, the enthralled body,

the charged and rocking and triumph-surging voice. . . .

People who have watched Miss Makeba's exciting performance on stage are always surprised, when they meet her in conversation, by her quiet, shy manner. Milton Bracker of *The New York Times*, interviewing her after her nightclub debut, in February, 1960, wrote:

> In daytime conversation Miss Makeba is so soft-spoken and reticent as to suggest a roll of extremely delicate paper ribbon. She can be unwound, but the most meticulous care must be exercised, lest the roll tear and the process have to begin all over again.

In a remark to another columnist (William McPherson of the *Washington Post and Times-Herald*), she explained it:

> I am African and I am black. I cannot speak what I feel. I can say what I feel only when I am singing. That's the only time I am happy.

But there came a time when she felt compelled to speak publicly. Already well known to the United Nations as a singer—through her performances on United Nations Day—she came before the UN Committee on Apartheid on July 16, 1963, to speak of her experience in South Africa. Describing the plight of Africans there as a "nightmare of police brutality and government terrorism," she asked for an international economic boycott of South Africa. Remembering her own relatives whom she had lost in the Sharpeville riot, she pleaded particularly against the shipment of arms which she had "not the slightest doubt will be used against African women and children." She came back to the UN the next year, this time to speak on behalf of jailed African leaders. Again she pleaded for the boycott, quoting words of a song written by the British actress, Vanessa Redgrave:

> You say you want to make me free—
> then don't trade with the men who are killing me.

Through the years Miss Makeba, like many others concerned about the lack of progress in combating apartheid, has been increasingly critical of the United States's economic involvement and failure to take a clear stand against government oppression of black people in South Africa. A number of important U.S. firms, among them General Motors, General Electric, Gulf Oil, Polaroid, and Chase Manhattan Bank, have heavy investments in South Africa; some individuals such as the New Jersey multimillionaire Charles Engelhard have grown enormously rich from their involvement there. As more information has become available, through Miriam Makeba and others, some Americans have begun to question the activities of these firms and individuals—not only from the standpoint of the distribution of profits (in which blacks share very scarcely), but also in terms of exploitation of blacks, a large source of the profits. Now, under increasing pressure from conscience-awakened Americans—some of whom are withdrawing investments in organizations doing business with South Africa—some of the U.S. firms are talking about changing their own labor policies, though South Africa's laws prevent them from changing the relative positions of blacks and whites. But few, if any, are ready to get out of South Africa.

As Miriam Makeba became an international star, it was difficult to keep track of her whereabouts. Sometimes exhausted by all the public acclaim and demand for her time, she would hide out somewhere for a few days with the help of friends. The apartment which she maintained, where her daughter Bongi eventually joined her, became a hospitality center for the growing number of South Africans coming to America; many of these could not, or would not, go home again.

"I'm going to Miriam's," a lonely student would say, on arriving in New York, and he knew he would find a welcome there—a meal, perhaps some old friends, and certainly some music from home.

There were other talented musicians arriving from South Africa, some of them no doubt encouraged by Miriam Makeba's success. Among them was the extraordinary trumpet player, composer, and singer Hugh Masekela. He and Miriam began performing together and eventually got married; however they were divorced only a few years later.

When Miriam Makeba married the Trinidad-born civil rights leader, Stokely Carmichael, in 1968, there was a lot of speculation. He was eight years younger, and had become a controversial figure in the United States; no longer head of SNCC, the civil rights organization he had helped to form, he was a black-power advocate increasingly at odds with the government, as well as with some of his fellow Afro-Americans. The Guinean ambassador, who cohosted the wedding reception in suburban New York with the ambassador from Tanzania, said the marriage was "the beginning of stronger ties between black people on both sides of the Atlantic." But Miriam saw it another way:

"People have given a number of reasons for our marriage," she said. "Oddly, no one has thought of love."

The wedding reception, postponed until three weeks after the actual wedding because of the death of Martin Luther King, was an extraordinary affair. According to an account in *Ebony* magazine (July 1968):

> The guest list testified to the unity theme of the event. It included representatives of free African nations, Afro-American

jazz musicians, black ghetto businessmen and militants, and a score of "the world's few decent white people."

It lasted four hours and included prayers to both deceased Africans and American slaves. Miriam herself led a combo and chorus through four South African songs, then sang a hymn beseeching her tribal ancestors to bless her marriage.

Since her marriage to Stokely Carmichael, Miriam Makeba has made her home in Conakry, Guinea, where she and her husband have found the atmosphere more congenial to their political interests. In addition to doing some English teaching there, Carmichael had been studying privately with Kwame Nkrumah, the exiled former president of Ghana, until Nkrumah's death in April, 1972.

Miss Makeba's appearances in the United States are less frequent these days, for various reasons. It is inevitable that a star with such a long international reputation should have her detractors. For a while some critics feared she was being smoothed up too much into a typical nightclub entertainer, losing her individual and natural African quality. Criticism lately has been that many of her performances are more political than musical. Among blacks everywhere there is growing controversy about how the liberation struggle should be waged—e.g., African nations today are at odds with each other on the matter of "dialogue" with South Africa (many feeling it hopeless—if not wrong—until blacks of South Africa can participate in the dialogue). Because of her more militant stand on this and other questions, Miriam Makeba has become unpopular in some of the more conservative countries. In Senegal recently her performance was canceled for this reason.

But such experiences do not dismay her. For, as she said in a recent interview, "I am happy because I am doing what I want to do."

Her daughter Bongi is married and has now given her two grand-

Miss Miriam Makeba is seen addressing the Special Committee on Policies of Apartheid.

children: a boy, named Lumumba for the Congolese leader who became an African liberation symbol in the early sixties, and a girl with the Xosa name of her grandmother, Zenzi.

The African songs introduced by Miriam Makeba that November night in 1959 have now become familiar to all Americans, through her own performances as well as the performances of many who learned them from her. One of her protégées, Letta Mbulu, a young South African woman, is establishing an international reputation of her own now. But for most people there is still no substitute for the original. When she is not available in person, Miriam Makeba's records are played: in homes, schoolrooms, in African boutiques, as back-

ground for festivals or protest rallies, sometimes for religious services.
. . . When she is available, people scream for Miriam to do their fa-
vorites: "Jikele Maweni!" "Nomeva!" "The Click Song!" "Wimoweh!" "Seven Years!" . . . There is never time to do them all, nor
will she stop until she has sung at least several freedom songs; some of
these are from Guinea, where she has done more recording lately.
The voice is as haunting and powerful as ever, the delivery even more
passionate.

In spite of the criticism of some for excessive militance, Miss Makeba's recent TV appearance with Nikki Giovanni reflected a spirit
of unusual tolerance and compassion. Tossing off her personal problems as unimportant, she had some words of wisdom for black Americans visiting Africa. She said they should not be surprised or hurt if
Africans do not immediately accept them as brothers; to many Africans the Afro hairdos and other attempts to dress in a special "African" way is puzzling and, to some, ridiculous. Reminding them that
American blacks had laughed at her short hair when she first arrived
in the United States, Miss Makeba said: "Be patient with your brothers." She then went on to predict that they would learn from each
other. Above all she pleaded for everyone to work for understanding
and mutual tolerance at deeper levels.

Because the lesson of mutual respect is still unlearned in her homeland, audiences in South Africa are still deprived of Miriam Makeba's
talents. But wherever she is Miss Makeba continues to "fight that
lion" and she remains hopeful that one day there can be a change.

She feels that African women can have a major role in effecting
that change.

"It is said that African women are the most backward, but this isn't
so!" she declared vehemently. "We can sit in the back seat and drive
the car."

ABOUT THE AUTHOR

LOUISE CRANE was born at Luebo, in the Kasai area of the former Belgian Congo, where her parents were American Presbyterian missionaries. She received her early education in the Congo, and earned her bachelor of arts degree from Queens College, Charlotte, North Carolina; her bachelor's of religious education from the Presbyterian School of Christian Education at Richmond, Virginia, and her master's of sacred music from Union Theological Seminary, New York.

Miss Crane, a teacher, writer, and lecturer, and author of *The Land and People of the Congo*, is currently doing research for the African Children's Project which has been undertaken by the New York State Education Department and funded by the National Endowment for Humanities.